PRAISE FOR DAVID

"David Deida must have the biggest balls in contemporary spirituality."

VIJAY RANA
—*The Watkins Review*

"As a woman, I've never felt so understood and validated."

MARCI SHIMOFF
—Co-Author of *Chicken Soup for the Woman's Soul*

"Every once in a while, someone comes along whose work is clearly a next step. Their ideas seem to answer some collective question hanging out in the culture. Their books and seminars become an underground buzz, and within a period of time, their ideas become part of our cultural vernacular. David Deida is such a person. In a time not too far off from now, his ideas will have spread like wildfire."

MARIANNE WILLIAMSON
—Author of *A Return to Love*

"There are few categories I know of for an original like David Deida; for his teachings there is no pigeonhole. He is a bridge-builder between East and West, between ancient and modern wisdom traditions. David Deida is in the dynamic living oral tradition of maverick spiritual teachers who, like free-jazz musicians, can riff directly on Reality, outside of established forms. Mark my words: in a future that I hope is not too far off, David Deida's original Western Dharma will be widely known as one of the most sublime and accessible expressions of the essence of spiritual practice that is freely offered today."

LAMA SURYA DAS
—Author of *Awakening the Buddha Within*

BLUE TRUTH

ALSO BY DAVID DEIDA

BOOKS

The Way of the Superior Man
A Spiritual Guide to Mastering the Challenges of Women, Work, and Sexual Desire

Dear Lover
A Woman's Guide to Men, Sex, and Love's Deepest Bliss

Intimate Communion
Awakening Your Sexual Essence

Finding God Through Sex
Awakening the One of Spirit Through the Two of Flesh

Wild Nights
Conversations with Mykonos about Passionate Love, Extraordinary Sex, and How to Open to God

The Enlightened Sex Manual
Sexual Skills for the Superior Lover

It's a Guy Thing
An Owner's Manual for Women

Instant Enlightenment
Fast, Deep, and Sexy

AUDIO

Enlightened Sex
Finding Freedom & Fullness Through Sexual Union

The Teaching Sessions: The Way of the Superior Man
Revolutionary Tools and Essential Exercises for Mastering the Challenges of Women, Work, and Sexual Desire

WEBSITE

www.deida.info

BLUE TRUTH

*A Spiritual Guide
to Life & Death
and Love & Sex*

DAVID DEIDA

Sounds True, Inc., Boulder, CO 80306

Originally published as *Naked Buddhism: 39 Ways to Free Your Heart and
Awaken to Now*, Plexus, 2002
Published 2005

ISBN 978-1-59179-259-8

10 9 8

Library of Congress Control Number: 2004098683

IMPORTANT CAUTION
Please Read This

Although anyone may find the practices, disciplines, and understandings in this book to be useful, it is made available with the understanding that neither the author nor the publisher are engaged in presenting specific medical, psychological, emotional, sexual, or spiritual advice. Nor is anything in this book intended to be a diagnosis, prescription, recommendation, or cure for any specific kind of medical, psychological, emotional, sexual, or spiritual problem. Each person has unique needs and this book cannot take these individual differences into account. Each person should engage in a program of treatment, prevention, cure, or general health only in consultation with a licensed, qualified physician, therapist, or other competent professional. Any person suffering from venereal disease or any local illness of his or her sexual organs or prostate gland should consult a medical doctor and a qualified instructor of sexual yoga before practicing the sexual methods described in this book.

TABLE OF CONTENTS

FOREWORD
by Lama Surya Das

How can I characterize *Blue Truth* and the spiritual teaching of David Deida?

David presents the kind of challenge that creative artists, spiritual awakeners, and innovators in the history of human beings have always posed. When faced with something new, original, and profound, language fails and the mind is humbled by the lack of a category to hang it on. I could compare David's work with the Tantric traditions that it certainly resembles in many respects—or Kashmir Shaivism ... Or I could write of its similarities with my own Dzogchen lineage of Buddhism, for it certainly shares with our tradition deep insights into reality and what is.

But there are few categories I know of for an original like David; for his teachings there is no pigeonhole. He himself is carving out his own territory, like a pioneer, an explorer. Unlike much of what we find in the spiritual marketplace today, David does not merely mouth pale shadows of truths from other times, places, and people, but is in the dynamic living oral tradition of maverick spiritual teachers who, like free-jazz musicians, can riff directly on Reality, outside of established forms. This is why I am attuned to his provocative, sacred music.

Naked awareness is the main practice in the Dzogchen traditition of Tibetan Buddhism. We take refuge in and rely on innate wakefulness and awareness practice to lay bare the nature of both the mind and all things; this is the ground, the path and the fruit of the tried and true Buddhist path of awakening. Awareness is the sovereign, all-powerful, and all-accomplishing ruler, the source of all; awareness is the greatest protection; awareness is the way, the truth, and the light. Homage to naked awareness, the heart of the Buddhas of past, present and future. David's book, *Blue Truth*, is such an homage.

Samantabhadara—embodying bare truth, naked awareness unencumbered by concepts—is the source of the Dzogchen lineage. Dzogchen actually predates the advent of Buddhism in Tibet. Dzogchen is also the consummate teaching of the Tibetan tradition, a nondual mystical transmission providing direct access to one's own innate natural state, the Buddha within. This primordial Buddha within us embodies the possibility of realization in one instant.

Thus Dzogchen pith instructions tell us: "One moment of total awareness is one moment of perfect enlightenment." This is the direct path, cutting directly to the core and touching truly upon the heart of the matter. This is what David Deida is transmitting and teaching. He comprehends these deep words. He practices these words by living them, and he teaches what he lives. He has an uncommon ability to render the most esoteric understandings at the core of the world's great spiritual wisdom in a form accessible and useful to the modern western mind.

David is a man with a mission; he is striving to transform the atmosphere of contemporary tantric teaching and practice in the world today. Although not a Buddhist or part of any pre-existing spiritual tradition, David Deida's fresh, original teaching lays bare the essence behind each moment's appearance. His is the exact form of on-the-spot insight, cutting through to the nature of reality, that traditions spring up in the wake of. But David is far more concerned with your authentic realization of openness and love than he is with creating more clothing for yet another spiritual outfit. His teaching serves to remove any cloaks your heart might be wearing, especially any garments knit of sexual confusion.

The true Buddha does not just sit above us all in the remote vastness of heavenly firmaments, but resides within the heart and mind of each and every one of us. What we seek, we are. It is all within. This is the naked truth, a veritable fact of life. David Deida understands this. He speaks from that position. To him, nakedness is far more than mere nudity, and his kind of tantra reaches far beyond prurient interests, sensuality, and mere sex.

From the primordial state of infinite, pure and spontaneously accomplishing awareness arises infinite teachings and manifestations. Timeless truths reveal themselves in timely new forms, appropriate for today and tomorrow. In our ancient Nyingma tradition of Tibet, these are called termas, or rediscovered Dharma treasures, which can come in the form of spiritual revelations of breathtaking beauty and grandeur as well as more pragmatically in the form of spiritual teachings and transmissions, empowerments, exercises and practices. This is how the Tibetan tantric Vajrayana tradition continues to revitalize and continually propagate itself. I believe that David Deida is actually onto something like this, in his own inimitable way.

These are big words, but David is a big mind that can step into such yeti-sized shoes and tread such a nondual mystical path. A gifted and charismatic teacher, an erudite and wise person of integrity and heart, David is the one western teacher of tantra whose books I read and whom I send students to learn from.

He is a bridge-builder between East and West, between ancient and modern wisdom traditions regarding this least understood of all spiritual teachings: the mystery of intimacy as a yoga of transformation, transcendence, and self-realization.

Buddha nature is the essence of every appearance and every moment of nowness. And *Blue Truth* points to the Buddha nature of now so artfully and so consistently, and in so many different areas of human life, that you can't help but have glimpses of the Dharmakaya, the Unborn and undying naked reality shining through your own experience, as you taste it via David's evocation of each moment's realization of what "is" in the very midst of what appears to be.

Blue Truth functions like the renowned Tibetan truth method called Pointing-out Instructions, reminding us that phantasmagorical visible appearances are a magical, dreamlike display of consciousness, energy, and light; and that the only authentic choice is to recognize it Just As Is within love's fearless, accepting embrace.

Mark my words: in a future that I hope is not too far off, David Deida's original western Dharma will be widely known as one of the most sublime and accessible expressions of the essence of spiritual practice that is freely offered today. The results of true practice, in any tradition, are unmistakable; David Deida demonstrates them.

Truths are many, but truth is one. All the great traditions have this truth at the core. Dzogchen teaching expresses it without much cultural accouterment or baggage. Not a matter of mere intellection, it can't really be taught—but it can be caught. When you catch on, then it is truly transmitted and realized. We can truly awaken in this way.

Spiritual seekers can realize what masters and sages throughout the ages have always realized: the facticity of what is, clear vision of things as they are through naked denuded awareness—not fabricating anything, not constructing, not building anything up, far beyond contrivance and elaboration. This true teaching on the primordially pure and perfectly whole, complete and radiant nature of reality, mind and consciousness is as true today as it was thousands of years ago.

No one has a corner on the market of truth. It is free and belongs to everyone, to one and all. Truth belongs to those who cherish it and realize it. Though David doesn't call himself a Buddhist, I do know that he is deeply rooted in Buddha nature. His teaching exposes that fact. I think we are all lucky to find these naked teachings here today, just as I count myself fortunate to have David as a Dharma friend.

Blue Truth is a fresh and original contribution to an unorthodox lineage tradition of unsullied new revelations. Much of the book helps us learn how to use our bare awareness and pure attention to reconnect and relax into the View of things as they are amidst daily life—with our kids, watching TV, at work and so forth. Beyond our time on the meditation cushion or yoga mat, spiritual awakening includes transcending our unfulfilling habitual conditioning, learning to love, and expressing our deepest heart in the midst of our everyday human lives. Sexuality in particular tends to hold people back from spiritual progress and development; the second half of this book is directed at transmuting this limitation into an opportunity, through skillful means of naked awareness practice and truth-method of self-realization.

So do me a favor. Let yourself rest loose, and read *Blue Truth* with the openness and freedom from preconceptions about Buddhism and religiosity that Zen masters call "beginners mind." When I read these oral teachings in written form, I like to remember the ancient Taost philosopher Chuang Tzu's advice, who said: "I am going to speak some reckless words, and I want you to listen recklessly." In that spirit, I can guarantee you that these insightful teachings will deepen your experience of immanent Buddha-nature and shine a new light on your moment-to-moment practice.

Lest we take all this too seriously, I find it helpful to remember that Buddha is as Buddha does. This is up to you. *Blue Truth* is about naked awareness: not something to believe in, but something to try out for yourself. As the Buddha himself used to say, "Come and see."

LAMA SURYA DAS
Dzogchen Center
Cambridge, Massachusetts
March 2002

Lama Surya Das is one of the foremost Western Buddhist meditation teachers and scholars. He is a lama in the Kagyu and Nyingma lineages of Tibetan Buddhism. His teachers include the Sixteenth Gyalwa Karmapa, Kalu Rinpoche, Dudjom Rinpoche, Dilgo Khyentse Rinpoche, Nyoshul Khenpo Rinpoche and Neem Karoli Baba. He has spent over thirty years studying Zen, vipassana, yoga, and Tibetan Buddhism, and has twice completed the traditional three year meditation retreat at Dilgo Khyentse Rinpoche's monastery in France. Surya Das is the founder of the Dzogchen Foundation in Massachusetts and California, founder of the Western Buddhist Teachers Network with the Dalai Lama, and is active in interfaith dialogue and social activism.

Lama Surya Das is also a poet, translator, chantmaster, and the author of the recently released *Awakening the Buddhist Heart: Integrating Love, Meaning, and Connection into Every Part of Your Life,* the bestselling *Awakening the Buddha Within,* and *Awakening to the Sacred.* He writes an "Ask The Lama" column online at Beliefnet.com. More information can be found at www.surya.org.

LIFE & DEATH

1

LOVE FULLY
AND DIE

❧

Sooner or later,
this present moment
is going to be your last.

You are alive, for now. Feel your heart beating in your chest. Soften your belly and relax your jaw. Feel your heart beating deep in your body, and feel your heart's rhythm radiating outward, pulsing in your hands and feet and neck. Feeling your heartbeat, relax open as if offering your heartbeat to the world.

While feeling your heartbeat as an offering to all, feel how you live your moments. What did you do today? What are your plans for tomorrow? Who do you love and how deeply?

No matter how much money or love you have made, one day your legs will become cold and numb, your heart will stop, your breath will cease, and all will disappear. In some now-moment as real as this present one, your life will end. Are you ready for your death? Are you ready for the death of your children, your parents, and your friends?

A picnic with your loved ones. Fried chicken and cold beer. A gentle breeze. Laughter. Suddenly your heart stops. A final glimpse. Fade to death.

Are you ready? Have you loved fully and given your deepest gifts?

A life lived well embraces death by feeling open, from heart to all, in every moment. Wide open, you can offer without holding back, you can receive without pushing away. Wide open, heart to all, you *are* openness, unseparate from this entire open moment. Every part of the moment comes and goes as openness.

Your daughter's smile: temporary, precious, already dissolving. Your lover's embrace: sweet, full, already loosening. Every moment is miraculous and disappearing. Every experience, profound and empty, both.

Life lived for the sake of experience is a half-life, tense, insecure, lonely, and unfulfilled. Your experience cannot fulfill you because as soon as it comes it is already gone, a thin wisp, the tail end of hope, receding out of reach.

Ungrasped, this moment of life burgeons free and bright. Surrendering wide, breathing deeply, offering your heart, you are birthed open as this moment. Death is permission to open freely as love.

2

FEEL BEFORE
MEMORY

〜∞〜

What is important
today is forgotten tomorrow.

When it's time to use the toilet, *really* time, all importance is reduced to the event.

In bed at *that* moment, orgasm is all.

Chased by a madman with a gun, there is *nothing* else; waking up from the dream, there is nothing else but *relief.*

A child finds her doll important. A father finds his finances important.

Riddled with cancer, an old man finds love important, as his eyes close one last time.

What do you find important, now, today? What did you find important ten years ago?

Remember back to your earliest childhood memory, the very first time you can remember anything at all. What was important to you then?

Still feeling your very first memory in life, feel *before* that. What happens when you try to feel earlier than your first memory? Do you feel into blackness? Is there a sharp wall of time that stops you? Or can you feel an ineffable openness that seems to extend before your earliest childhood memory, an openness without clear bounds, an openness that is you even now?

Of every moment that has ever seemed important, all that remains is the openness who you are.

3

GIVE EVERYTHING
NOW

∽⧜

You are either withholding
your love in fear or
giving your deepest gifts.

Right now, and in every now-moment, you are either closing or opening. You are either stressfully waiting for something—more money, security, affection—or you are living from your deep heart, opening *as* the entire moment, and giving what you most deeply desire to give, without waiting.

If you are waiting for *anything* in order to live and love without holding back, then you suffer. Every moment is the most important moment of your life. No future time is better than now to let down your guard and love.

Everything you do right now ripples outward and affects everyone. Your posture can shine your heart or transmit anxiety. Your breath can radiate love or muddy the room in depression. Your glance can awaken joy. Your words can inspire freedom. Your every act can open hearts and minds.

Opening from heart to all, you live as a gift to all. In every moment, you are either opening or closing. Right now, you are choosing to open and give fully or you are waiting. How does your choice feel?

Unfold
Your Heart

 ❧

The way that you live
is probably not
your true destiny.

How would you live if you were fearless, if you lived your life as an expression of your deepest heart?

As an act of unrestrained love, you might become a mother, a politician, or a writer. Perhaps you would invent a vaccine, create a business, or perform music. You might become a farmer, a teacher, or an attorney. Love moves each person in a different way.

The way love moves you is your true destiny. When you don't add fear to love's force, your life unfolds unimpeded. Each day is a flowering of your deepest gifts. At work, with your family, and alone, each moment springs open from the depths of your heart.

How can you allow your true destiny to unfold? In this moment, allow your breath to be full, strong, and tender, as if pressing love from your deep belly into the softness of your lover. Relax your muscles, open your senses, and feel into the world around you, as if feeling into the light of a dream, breathing this light in and out. From your deep heart and soft belly, offer love outward in all directions as far as you can open to feel. Your true destiny unfolds freely when you live every moment open and shine as an offering of love.

However, if you add fear to your life—as most people do—then your moments take the shape of your cringe. Anxiety about money clips the artistry of your career. Fear of loss stifles honesty with your lover. Your gut tenses because you don't really want to be where you are. Fear is the opposite of love.

Few men or women live their true destiny. Most follow a trajectory bent by fear. Your true destiny is lived by giving everything and loving open without waiting.

If you wait to open fully, then your heart aches as your life curls in the shape of your chosen consolations. Your bedtime snuggles and TV rituals can assuage your pangs of unlived love for a while, but your heart's pain of closure slowly accumulates to unbearable.

Sometimes a crisis exposes your heart fully open. Your business unexpectedly fails. Your child becomes terminally ill. Stripped of what you most cherish, you are left out in the open and unprotected.

One way or another, you come to face the truth: Everything you acquire is eventually lost. Every body you hold eventually dies. You have been waiting to give your deepest gifts, waiting to love without holding back, while your life—everyone's life—passes. You have bartered your true destiny for false comfort and muted agony.

You can stop waiting. When you are ready, you can intentionally breathe open as the *full* truth: Love is who you are. This moment is as open as you are willing to be. All your guarded moments are life wasted.

You can start opening fully now. If you feel fear, if you are waiting for more security or comfort, if you are holding back your gifts or closing down your love, then feel your act of closure fully. Feel the tension in your muscles, the clenching of your jaw, the hardening around your heart. Feel fear's shape, in your muscles, emotions, and life choices. Feel the brightness of the moment constrained by your apprehension. As you feel yourself doing the shape of fear, breathe more fully, in and out.

As you inhale, expand your belly more fully, filling your deep gut with love's light and energy. Then, as you exhale, offer love outward to all, relaxing your muscles open, feeling out into the colors of the world as you continue breathing. Feel others more deeply. Feel their hearts' longing and joy as you breathe their aliveness in and out of your heart. As if breathing the light of a dream, breathe the aliveness of the entire moment in and out. Continue opening, feeling all, breathing all, loving open, allowing your actions to unfold as your deepest offering.

When fear returns, which it probably will, feel the shape of your closure. Feel your fear, feel everyone's fear and darkness. Inhale everyone's fear deep into your open heart and exhale love's open light as an offering. Relax and feel everyone so openly that you feel *as* everyone, as their shape, as their fear, as their deep heart's love. As everyone, open and breathe. As the shape of the entire moment, open and breathe. If closure remains, feel, breathe, and open again, without end.

Your true destiny is lived by opening as love and offering your deepest gifts, moment by moment. How you do this—as a mother of three children, as a hermit in a cave, or as a political leader—is for you to discover as each moment unfolds open as unimpeded love.

If you have opted for a life shaped by imagined security, you can feel your true destiny in your heart, waiting to be lived, wanting to open as the offering of your life. As you breathe open and offer your deepest gifts of love, your life can flower afresh. As you slowly open your heart's cringe, your business may show a new style. Your sexual depth may open to your lover more fully. Anything can happen as your heart unfurls and your moments open wide as love.

Your true destiny may seem far less predictable than the imitation you have spent years holding in place. The choice is yours in every moment. You can hold the shape of a consoling lifestyle for decades. It only costs your life.

5

RESIST
NOTHING

≈

Opening as every moment
is the practice of true bliss.

T he human body is very sensitive to pain. Stub your toe, and for a few
moments you are consumed in minor agony. Emotionally, too, pain is
ever possible. Your lover betrays you, and your heart feels crushed. When you
feel the agony of lost love—let alone the immense suffering of the world's
starving and dying millions—you can be wracked with sorrow.

Feeling physical and emotional pain is natural and inevitable, but
uncomfortable. So you do what you can to avoid it. You can drive a nice
car, isolate yourself from diseased and wretched people, and minimize
rocking the boat of your intimate relationship. Your effort to avoid pain is
as natural as pain itself.

Most of your life can become the effort to avoid pain, to experience pleasure, and to pretend everything is OK, even though something feels amiss.
Your life can still feel incomplete, even in the midst of a fine meal with a smiling lover at the peak of health.

Even during the best of times, you may suffer a sense of lack. This dissatisfaction occurs because you are not opening. When you open fully as any moment, you are complete. Your broken arm may still ache. Your heart may still reel in response to the loss of someone you love. But if you practice opening now, then you add less self-created suffering to life's natural fluctuation of pleasure and pain.

Feel your pleasure, or its lack, right now. If you are feeling relatively comfortable, for instance, then notice that you can *feel* your comfort. You are open to feeling your comfort. Your openness is what allows you to feel your comfort.

Now, your comfort has changed a bit. Your posture has shifted slightly. Your tongue or fingers may have moved. What you feel now is slightly different than what you felt a moment ago—but that you can feel at all means you are *open* to feeling.

Fully open, and as openness, feel. Allow your tongue to open and feel. Allow your fingers to open and feel. Feel the entire surface of your skin open to sensation. Feel your mind open to thoughts. Feel your eyes open to light. Whatever you are feeling—however painful or pleasurable—you can feel it because you are *open*.

Regardless of how much pain or pleasure the moment brings you, the truth is that you *are* openness. When you resist any aspect of the moment, when you close to an emotion, a person, or a situation, then you deny the openness you are. You create separateness and suffering—you *do* separateness and suffering—even though you may be sitting in a hot tub with a beautiful lover eating grapes.

Pleasure and pain come and go, and there is only so much you can do about it. To be born is to be guaranteed some amount of enjoyment, discomfort, and certain death. Simply to be alive as a body is to know both health and disease. To enjoy intimacy is to expose your heart to deep sharing as well as to the unloving moments of others. True bliss is to remain open—as you are—in the midst of all experience, both heavenly and hellish.

Regardless of how much comfort you are experiencing, you can surrender open as you are or you can knot yourself closed. If you open as you are now, a spacious and tender love abides—the openness that *is* feeling—even if your body aches or your lover has spurned you. If you close now, turning in on yourself in an effort to avoid exposure, then you suffer your own separative cramp, even if you are surrounded by love.

Openness is bliss, though not the giddy kind of bliss you feel when someone tickles you. When you feel anything, you are open as feeling. Openness is who you *are*, your most fundamental feeling of being. When you close to the moment, resisting emotions, people, or situations, then you deny your openness, and you suffer. Openness is bliss because it is most deeply who you are.

Your heart always knows the truth of openness. In every moment of your life, your heart tacitly compares the closed suffering that you are *doing* to the bliss of your true openness. "This moment can be deeper." "Our love can be more full." "My life can be more fulfilling." Your heart knows the truth of openness and suffers the tense lie of your closure.

Chronic dissatisfaction is how you sense that you are living this lie. No matter how much pleasure or pain comes your way, dissatisfaction means you are resisting the openness of the moment, the openness who you are, the truth. When you are not open to emotions, people, and situations, then you are denying your most basic nature, the openness who you are.

Practice being openness by opening to feel. Just as you are, even though you may have habits of closure, you can always practice opening to feel. Open to feel whatever you are feeling now. Open to feel your breath moving in and out, feel the posture of your body, feel the space and motion in the room around you, feel the emotional tone of the people nearest to you. Open and feel. Open as feeling. Open to feel everything, and feel as openness itself.

In the midst of orgasm, practice opening, breathing and feeling all that you can feel, your intense pleasure, your lover, the entire room, the lives beginning and ending everywhere, and continue opening to feel everything fully without closure. In the aftermath of a car accident, practice breathing and feeling everything, your cuts and bruises, your fear, the love of those who care for you, and continue to feel open as each moment unfolds, pain and all.

Do your best to create pleasure and comfort in your life. But to live true, live open. Resist nothing. Feel everything. Breathe everyone's pain and pleasure in and out of your heart. If you feel a lack in your life, practice living and breathing and feeling open.

Openness is truly who you are.

6

BREATHE
EVERYTHING

∽

*Your suffering is shaped
exactly by your refusal to open.*

Most of your life is beyond your control. The hour of your death, who you will meet during your life, your wealth and your health are partially in your hands, but mostly far beyond any influence you can exert. Chance, synchronicity, and an invisible web of influences—everything from world events to childhood traumas to subtle energetic forces—form a confluence of patterns that appears as the days of your life.

Your intent and decisions are certainly part of this web of influence, too, but they are circumscribed by immense past-future patterns, of which only a tiny slice is presently visible. Your best intentions and most careful decisions can lead to utter devastation or glory, depending on this or that and things you can't see. In any case, you can only do your best. The rest is out of your hands.

How trapped you feel by your life, however, is entirely a matter of your depth of openness. To the extent that you close and pull back from your experiences, you feel separate. To the extent that you close and protect your heart, you feel alone. To the extent that you close to your deepest desire and opt for security, you feel disempowered.

Open deeply, and you are free. Close yourself, and you feel trapped. You build your own traps through your patterns of closure.

You can be lying in bed, sick and near death. Do everything within your power to heal, and also open as you are. Feel your aching. Is it sharp or dull pain? Is it constant or throbbing? Does it move or stay still? Does it feel black or green or red? Feel your aches in great detail, as if you were an artist of pain, feeling into pain's texture, opening to feel its essence.

To feel fully is to open fully. Feel your disease fully, like a mother feeling an infant's needs, or like a golfer feeling the wind, distance, and direction as he swings to hit the ball. Open and feel. Feel and open. As openness, your actions spring from your depth. In every moment of opening and feeling without closure, you are alive as love. The more open you allow yourself to feel, the more free you are in your art, parenting, golfing—or illness.

Whether you open or close makes all the difference to whether you feel trapped by your situation or open as an offering of love. As you do your best to heal, also do your best to open, or else even health will feel less than free. Many healthy people feel trapped by their lives. Health and sickness are both possible; health is better. But only openness fulfills your deepest longings to be free and alive as love.

The contour of your closing, the form of your suffering, is defined by what you won't embrace, feel, and open as. If you won't embrace and open as your mother's rejection of you, then it defines your quiet anguish. If you won't embrace and open as your fear of success, then it will define your impotent recoil. If you won't embrace and open as your desire to be ravished, then it will define your tense armor.

You are trapped by that which you feel partially, recoil from, and refuse to *be* as openness. If you feel anything *fully*—even your mother's hate or your own bodily pain—then you can feel *as* it, open as it, and live free amidst hurt. You can feel into and *as* your mother's spite, her anguish, her fear, and her loneliness, just as you can feel into and *as* your searing innards, your burning skin, and your faltering breath.

When you notice yourself resisting, practice feeling fully and opening. If your mother's hate tortures you, feel "Yes" rather than "No." Breathe in her hate. Feel her hate through your whole body, down to your toes. Soften your belly, taste her hate, smell her hate, become her hate. Be her hate as fully as you can, and open *as* her hate. Relax your body, open your heart, breathe fully, and feel outward as her hate.

You are a connoisseur, tasting hate. A dancer, dancing as hate. A ray of light, shining as hate. A river, flowing as hate. A bubble, bursting as hate. Hate? "Yes." Feel hate, be hate, open as hate.

Otherwise, hate traps you in the form of your closure. You feel your mother's hate—or your own body's pain—and you close down. Your breath constricts, your belly tightens, your muscles tense. You make decisions based on this closure, and so your life adheres to closure's contour. The only way to live free, the only way to live your life as an offering of love, is to feel everything fully and live open.

Closed, feeling "No" to some aspect of your experience, your world shrinks to the size of your refusal's clench. You become enclosed in the tightness of your "No," unaware of the openness beyond the drama of your contraction. Instead, you can fully feel your closure, breathe fully the texture of your pain, and open *as* whatever you are feeling, in any moment. Open and alive as love, you are free.

Freedom doesn't mean freedom *from*. As long as you are alive, you can never be free from pain, from loss, or from death. Things come and go, including your loved ones and your own body and mind. True freedom means freedom *as*. True freedom is to feel fully and be alive as love, feeling *as* this entire moment, opening just as this moment is.

If you feel depressed by your life's failures, then allow yourself to truly feel what depression is. Feel your sunken chest, your shallow breath, your maudlin emotions. Notice your attention adhering inside the shape of your collapse, and feel wider.

Feel ten feet wider than your sulking body, so you can feel the room or space around you. Open your feeling wider, so you can feel out beyond the building you are in. Listen for the farthest sound you can hear. Feel even farther, so that your feeling-heart opens to feel outward to infinity.

Breathe infinity, the openness of feeling, in and out of your heart. Feel the moment alive; everything is changing, shifting, shining. Feel the livingness of your world, your emotions, and your mind—all alive and displaying like a fantastic dream.

Open and feel all of the display, inside and outside, as deep and as wide as you can feel. Breathe as the livingness of the full display, feeling and opening as the entire moment—however depressed your body, mind, and emotions may seem.

Do your best to help others and to improve your own life, knowing that, for the most part, it is quite out of your hands. As you intend, decide, and act to the best of your ability, practice living open.

When you feel trapped by life, take it as a sign that you are clenched within the confines of your own "No." You are refusing some experience, resisting some person, or trying to avoid some feeling. Trapped within this recoil, even your most generous intentions are knotted by fear's tension.

Instead, embrace fully in your heart's "Yes" whatever you are refusing. Feel your shape of tension, relax as it, and feel open, ten feet at a time, eventually feeling from your heart to all, and beyond. Breathe as the shape you may still be holding, and breathe open as the all-living light, alive as the entire moment's display. As everything comes and goes, live all things open as love, gifting without choice from your depth. Freedom is openness is love.

7

WEAR
EVERYONE'S SHAPE

∽

You are giving others
the gift of your openness
or the clench of your refusal.

A re you utterly fulfilled, right now? If so, then you are unmoved by stress, and your life unfolds as openness. But if you are not totally fulfilled, then you feel a strange lack. When this "something missing" motivates you, then you create suffering in the world, for everyone you know, and for yourself.

You are probably, to some extent, being moved by this feeling of essential lack: you want more security, more affection, more understanding. Also, to some extent, you are opening as love; your thoughts and actions are spontaneously welling up from your open heart of depth. That is, you are living some percentage of your life as clench and some percentage as gift.

Spiritual growth involves living more and more of your life as an offering of love. As you learn to open as every moment, your life springs from the open love who you are at depth. When you live as love, then you give love to the world, resonating others so they, too, open and begin to live as love.

To the extent that you are closed, you give stress to the world. Your clench ripples outward, resonating others into closure. Even when you try to help others, your clench communicates itself along with your efforts. People may benefit from your actions, but in the process they are also rippled by your clench.

Your service is only entire when your actions arise as love, emerging through a body lived as openness. And the only way to live as openness is to *feel* as openness. You can practice feeling each moment as it is and open as its form.

For instance, when you are confused, you can practice opening as confusion. You can actually feel the texture of confusion, wear it like a perfectly fitted suit, and relax as its shape, open. Open as you are, you can feel outward to feel and open as the entire moment. No matter how lousy you feel inside, you can open as your shape. Just as you are—confused, clumsy, bewildered—you can practice feeling outward, bit by bit, and open as all.

Opening as this moment is utter fulfillment. You can practice feeling open as all, starting with feeling and opening as the specific shape of your posture, breath, movement, thoughts, emotions, and actions. Alive as openness, every part of you and all of your life is fulfilled—fully experienced as love and fully dissolved as love.

Any aspect of this moment that remains is yours with which to practice. If confusion persists, then you can practice by persisting to wear confusion, feeling its shape, breathing as confusion, moving as confusion, and actually opening *as* confusion, right now, to feel outward, finally breathing and opening as the entire moment, again and again. You are alive as the breath-action-feeling that is confusion, and you open as its entire shape to feel outward to all, like a soap bubble opening as wide as the sunlight, again and again and again.

Living each moment open, you bless the world. Your openness begets openness. Those around you resonate open, to the extent they are ready. And, just like you, they aren't always ready for much.

Anything you are not willing to experience and open as, you will repeatedly confront. If you are afraid to feel anger, if you are unwilling to love as anger and dissolve open as anger, then you will continually struggle with anger in yourself and others. If you are afraid to feel, love, and open as insecurity, then you will necessitate threats to your security. Your very recoil will sustain the ripples of that which you fear, necessitating a confrontation with whatever you are unwilling to fully feel, be alive as, and open as.

Suppose you see a fat person on TV who has an eating problem. Can you feel yourself as a fat person with an eating problem? Can you actually become the stress of the eating problem, feel your weight, your craving, your loneliness? Can you feel this shape altogether and open as love while being this shape?

You can open as every form of experience. If you do not—if you close down, pull away, or keep your distance from fully feeling some experience—then you will perpetuate its pattern, its ripples of closure. If you cannot open as love while you "wear" the entire shape of a fat person with an eating problem, then this pattern will continue in isolation, unloved and separate, clenched closed.

And you will feel the same. You are the openness of this entire moment, and you feel every separative tension whether it seems to belong to you or someone else.

As openness, you open as every being. As openness, you are actually responsible for the openness of everyone. Walking down the street, you pass an old man in a wheel chair. Can you feel his shape? Can you breathe his raspy squeak of a breath? Can you feel death nearby, youth behind, and stretched-out days of gurgle, pain, and disintegration? Feeling his entire pattern of being, can you open *as* this old man? Can you open as love, feeling every nuance of his decrepit form as the basis of your opening?

Until you can open as the form of everyone, your depth—love itself—remains unopen. You will remain deeply unfulfilled, and others will be rippled by the clench of your closure.

First, you can practice opening as your own shape, whatever it is in the moment: anger, joy, confusion, fear, grief, torpor.

After practicing for some time, your openness is, in general, more open than those around you—their clench hurts you more than your own does. Now, you can't help but to practice opening as *their* shape. Just as you feel them, you open. If they feel angry, you open as anger. If they feel lustful, you open as lust. You practice fully feeling and opening as every texture you feel.

It doesn't matter if the closure you feel is yours or theirs. Opening is the only response that ceases to perpetuate the clench you feel.

Your life, then, is a constant exercise of opening as the entirety of the moment. Whoever or whatever is part of this moment, you feel as and open as. You practice opening as whatever you feel, within you or around you, in every moment.

Some moments are easier than others. Sometimes you don't want to open. You may prefer to chew on closure, to perseverate on possibility, to convolute in emotion. These moments are unfulfilling but habitual. Sometimes it seems you can't help but writhe in the folds of your own tension.

You and all others are exactly the same. You and they are openness, often choosing to stay clenched. It seems that each clench has its own timeline. You can't force yourself or others to suddenly open all the way and stay open once and for all. Certain parts open easily, while others seem to refuse. Perhaps you can dance as openness or meditate as openness, but when someone criticizes your great work or loses desire for you sexually, then you simply refuse to open. Like a pouting child, you refuse to feel every texture of your shame, hurt, and insecurity; you refuse to open *as* this shape, to feel outward, to feel others, to feel the entire moment, and open as all.

You are fulfilled in any moment you practice to open, no matter how closed you are tending to be, or whose closure you feel. Practicing to open as the shape of this entire moment is the only response that is true.

You are either living open as love or clenching. You are either living the truth of openness or you are living a lie of closure—and deep down, you can feel it.

Love, or openness, is the gift you are to others. Your capacity to live as openness conveys your depth of love. When you can wear everyone's closure as the shape of this moment, and when you can open as these contours of refusal, feeling and opening as all, then no residue of unlove remains. Even if clench is redone, its action of fear is well felt, and openness blooms through its form afresh. Every moment reveals open as love. This is your only fulfillment.

8

OFFER YOURSELF
AS LOVE

~

*You look like
what you feel.*

Whatever you pay attention to, right now, you begin to look like. Whatever you have spent time attending to in the past, you already look like.

What would a videotape show if you had been recorded for the last eight hours? Would your face be long or glowing? Would your chest be sunken or beaming? Would you move like a nervous robot or an ebullient lover?

Suppose you sit at a computer all day, staring into the screen, pushing around words and numbers. Day after day, your body and mind resonate with cyberspace. You can easily begin to look like the dry domain to which you have been attending: functional, logical, insensate. Your shoulders can become hunched, your head tight, your body vacant. Feeling into a computer day after day can de-vitalize you.

Or, suppose your lover leaves you, and you spend the day mulling over the breakup, feeling hurt, depressed, and afraid. Your chest caves in, your breath becomes shallow, your face waxes pallid. You begin to look like the domain of dark and sagging emotional energy to which you have been attending. Feeling into gloomy sentiments, your entire demeanor is endarkened.

Imagine that you've just won a million dollars. Your eyes widen, your face flushes, you dance and scream and whoop, hugging everyone around you. You look like the domain of abundant energy to which you now attend, thanks to your million-dollar moment. Feeling into the huge flow of money invigorates you.

Where you put your attention defines how you look and feel. For instance, you could attend to your genital need. You could go to a party and put your attention on potential sexual partners. Eventually, if all you did was place your attention on sex, you would begin to look and feel like a genital with arms and legs. And if you go to a singles bar, you may indeed see a number of walking, talking genitals.

On the other hand, right now, you can feel into the deepest love in your heart. You can remember someone you truly love, or you can simply feel directly into your deep heart, attending to its openness, compassion, and care. You can do this through the day. Even when something upsets you, you can choose to put your attention on your heart, and feel into the domain of love.

Feel the beating of your heart now. Relax your body and soften your breath so you can feel your deep heart beating and pulsing outward to your hands and feet and head. Imagine opening your chest so your heart was exposed to the world without protection, glistening, alive, tender. Imagine offering your beating heart as a gift to all, like offering a vibrant, delicate flower to your lover.

Opening your heart to all, feel your offering as love. What does love feel like? How does love show? As you feel your beating heart and open outward to all, what would a videotape of you reveal?

When you consistently open as love, you begin to look like love. Your face shines. Your eyes sparkle. Your body moves with grace, opening as the tide of love swelling from your deep heart to all—through the day, at work, during sex. Your voice carries the fullness of love rather than the stress of genital need or the exasperation of emotional betrayal. Since every part of you takes on the characteristic of what you feel, if you feel as love you show as love.

You can attend only to your worried thoughts and troubled emotions, and therefore appear as a twisted and fearful character. Or, even when you are worried or troubled, you can feel open as an offering of love.

Through this practice of feeling open, history evaporates as it occurs. Openness prevails. Love appears as you.

9

UNCLENCH AS
IF ASLEEP

∽

*Fear underlies
most of your life.*

In deep, dreamless sleep, there is no fear. Otherwise, fear swirls through your thoughts, emotions, and body for most of your day and night. You are afraid of poverty so you work to earn money. You are afraid of loneliness so you try to secure intimacy. You are afraid of relaxing without a future so you think, and think, and think.

Fearless ease is precious. Fear abates momentarily when you forget yourself in a sunset, a child's laughter, or a warm bath. Your mind opens, your heart unstresses, your body eases in pleasure. But soon, in response to a whiff of threat, imagined or real, you tense up. Your mind reels, your emotions churn, your body tightens. After a while, fear feels normal. Shallow breath? Tight jaw? Incessant thinking? Hey, that's life, it seems.

Life seems to be suffering. You are constantly plotting, rehearsing conversations, living in apprehension. Your gut is knotted. Your heart is hardened. Deep sleep is just about the only time you aren't mulling, cogitating, or dreaming. Deep sleep feels like a dunk into unperturbed bliss, a restoration of easeful depth and seamless openness. And then, as the alarm clock rings, your belly tightens and your mind begins wheeling again.

Remain sensitive as you emerge from deep sleep into wakeful stress. With gentle openness, feel the deep, silent peace abiding beneath the swirl of emerging thoughts, sounds, colors, and feelings. Waking life is an *addition* to the depth of sleep's bliss. In any moment, you can feel into the province of sleep's deep openness, even now. The silent heart-hum of deep sleep lies beneath the flash of present occurrence, like a deep sea of peace below a hectic churn of waves.

Fear keeps your mind on the waves. Fear is a tension: What will happen if I stop paying attention to everything that needs to be done?

What *does* happen if you surrender as if in deep sleep, right now? What happens if you allow action and perception to well up from open depth, without effort, spontaneously springing from this source?

Virtually everything that happens has nothing to do with your conscious intent. Your food is digested, metabolized, and distributed throughout your body without your volition. Your heart beats, your breath swells, even your thoughts occur spontaneously, like dreams throughout the day, and then disappear without your interference. Your life is an assemblage of arising processes, and your awareness is more or less along for the ride.

Yet there is a sense of continuous I-ness. As waking takes form on the bliss of deep sleep, you have probably been, for a brief moment, aware of your attention rising from sleep's silent depth, enfolding in the show of waking drama. With practice, you can relax as the source of sleep's depth even while awake. All your thinking, emoting, and acting can be felt taking form as part of this vast openness of being, like vortexes forming on the surface of deep water.

Close your eyes for a moment, and allow yourself to sink down and inward, as if going to sleep. Feel the place deep within that is silent, boundless, and utterly stress-free. Relax into this place as if you were easing into the deepest sleep. When you feel this silent depth of blissful feeling, as if deep asleep, then open your eyes.

With your eyes now open, continue to feel your depth, the place where sleep abides. Feel the unending openness, the deep water of your heart, and continue opening. Feel the world around you as if appearing to you in deep sleep. Open to the colors you see. Open to the sounds you hear. Open to the people around you.

While feeling as sleep's depth opening out to all, also open as your body. Feeling open down deep, while also opening to everything and everyone around you, allow action to spring from your deep belly. Do not move until an impulse to do so grows out from your depth.

When the impulse to move stirs in your guts, then move while feeling open from depth to all. As if deep asleep, eyes wide open, feeling all others and things as they are, allow yourself to open and feel and move as love's offering from your deep belly. Live as love open from depth to all.

From depth, you can live all your days open as love. But without this connection to your deep source, you are creased by fear's hesitation. Your life is conflicted by surface waves, crisscrossed by opposing tensions, needs, and wants, occasionally smoothed by brief pleasures. You may smile, but death awaits you, deep love eludes you, and the freedom of final victory is unachieved.

Feel your terror of *completely* letting go, just as you are, right now. While feeling this essential fear, open deeper than fear. Practice feeling open as the deep source and textured substance of this moment. Be the water, feeling open from depth through your life's surface currents and out beyond the moment's open verge. Practice feeling open all day, as love's unclenched offering.

10

Relax as
You Are

❧

Self-improvement
is better than
shame but less mature
than openness.

You can grow in your approach to negative emotions.
As you start to become more self-aware, you may notice yourself wallowing in negativity, even as you deny you have a problem. Negative emotions clearly drain your energy. They drag you down. Hate, anger, lust, depression, greed—it is better to be loving, compassionate, creative, and generous, or so it seems.

So you grow to the next stage. You dedicate yourself to self-improvement. You can use many methods to transform your negative emotions into positive ones. You can go to a therapist and discover the root of your anger in childhood. You can learn to reframe your experience, so when anger comes up, you visualize the best moment of your life and swish a new pattern of emotion into the moment. Instead of wallowing in anger, you can learn to transform anger into positive motivation.

Instead of hating someone, you learn to feel sympathy for him or her, knowing that as evil as they seem, they are suffering just like you, searching for an answer. Rather than festering in envy, you grow to feel abundance—how wonderful it is that beauty is overflowing everywhere and through everyone. When a negative emotion comes up, instead of denying it, getting tense, and stuffing your face with food or alcohol, you can learn various ways to transform heavy emotions into positive and energetic motivations and feelings.

You used to feel ashamed of yourself, and now you feel good about yourself. Eventually, however, if you continue to grow, your desire to transform negative emotions into positive ones begins to feel false. Your need to feel good about yourself begins to be a burden. Your need to feel successful, lovable, and unique begins to feel unnecessary, like a scab ready to fall off. Just as you were once motivated to feel good rather than bad, now you are naturally ready to open without any self-image—positive or negative—to protect you from what *is*.

As you grow spiritually, your approach to negative emotions naturally matures. First, you flounder in negativity, alternating between denial and shame. Then, you embark on a well-intentioned effort to transform negative emotions into positive ones, improving yourself so that you become a more successful and lovable person in the mirror of your self-worth.

Finally, you can't help but live true to what is, *whatever* is. You stop trying to buoy yourself with motivation and positive thinking. You open as the lack and the darkness you sometimes feel. You are willing to feel, breathe, and be *everything*, dark and light. Opening in every now-moment, your life is no longer lived as a hope for success and love, but as an unfolding openness.

Suppose you feel down about yourself. You feel unworthy. So, you decide to use an affirmation in order to brighten your sense of self: "I deserve love and success. I am a unique, powerful, and worthy person."

Affirmations can work for a while, but eventually, if you continue growing, affirmations can begin to feel thin. Your feeling grows deeper, and under it all, in spite of your efforts, you sense you are still nothing. How can you work with your depression and continue growing?

If you are willing to feel exactly what is and open as you are, then your life unfolds as truth. For instance, if you feel you are nothing, then open as nothing, fully.

"I'm nothing," you feel. Relax into the pit of nothingness. Allow yourself to sink into the blackness. Feel dark nothingness seeping through your skin, pervading your body, blackening through your heart and gut. Breathe and relax and open as dark nothingness.

You are openness alive as black. Continue opening as you are, feeling outward in all directions without bounds.

As darkness, breathe and feel open. Allow the moment to unfold open, as you are.

If you feel anger, then be willing to feel anger completely. Feel your face flushing red and your heart beating hard. Feel your hands balling into fists while your feet want to stomp. Feel hot energy coursing up from your belly, bulging your eyes, wanting to shout from your mouth.

Feel your entire body alive as anger, and open to feel around you. While alive as anger, feel into the ground, into the sky, and outward into every direction. Feel into any person you are with. If your lover made you angry, feel into your lover. Look into your lover's eyes. Feel into your lover's heart. Open your heart to feel every part of yourself and your lover.

From your heart, open as anger, breathe as anger, feel anger course through your body, feel into your lover, and open. Feel your lover's heart, your lover's breathing, your lover's energy, and also open wider than your lover. Feel the energy of the wind, of the sun, of everyone everywhere. Feel anger and open, feel your lover and open, feel all and open, from heart through all and beyond.

Unfold open as anger without bounds, feeling all from the open depth of your heart.

If you feel lust, feel it completely. Open your heart to feel the fire in your loins. From your deep heart, feel your want, your need, your urgency to merge, to consume, to be consumed. Lust fully and without stopping short.

Alive as lust, urgent and hungry to be satisfied, feel from your heart into the yummy one you desire. Breathe deliciousness in and out. Feel and breathe the fullness of her lips, the roundness of her butt. Feel and breathe the intensity in his eyes, the strength in his spine. Feel and breathe the chocolate of the cake, the coolness of the beer. Feel and breathe, in and out, the luscious object of your lust, fully.

From your heart, feel through your lustful body to its object, and now open to feel as far as you can. As lust alive, feel from your heart to your left and your right, behind and in front of you, downward and upward, feeling outward in every direction as far as you can. Alive as lust, feel outward without limits. Open without end, from your heart, as lust, feeling all you desire fully, breathing all you desire in and out, feeling outward further to open beyond the horizon of the moment.

Open as whatever so-called negative emotion you feel. Open as you are, whatever you are feeling. Whatever you are feeling, open. Live as love, feeling outward without horizon. Feeling all, breathing all, open exactly as you are.

Every moment, no matter how bad or good, is unfolding open. The hope for personal success and positive emotion is most fascinating when you have forgotten, or have yet to discover, the endless opening you are.

11

HONOR
YOUR DEPTH

❧

*If you want to change
your life fundamentally,
try going deeper before forcing
yourself to behave differently.*

Y ou have probably made New Year's resolutions that you haven't kept. Perhaps
you have promised to change your diet, to exercise more, or to stick to a plan
of action, only to fail. You start off strong but eventually fall back into old habits,
unable to continue on the path envisioned by your initial inspiration.

Actually, you have very little control over your life. Your thoughts and feelings
can be intentionally shaped to some degree, but mostly you are a creature com-
posed of habit. You can set new habits in motion, but few stick. Soon, you are back
to your old patterns. Your personal characteristics can be smoothed around the
edges, but for the most part your attributes are carved in flowing stone.

Your life is carved by patterns and forces playing far beyond your awareness and intention. At night, your dreams are spun without volition. During
the day, you think and act in ways that are often contrary to what you intend.
Seemingly random meetings and events can change the course of your entire
life. Somehow it all hangs together, but it's tough to see the pattern that con-
nects all the aspects of your life.

No matter how dearly you try to control, your life unfolds as a mystery. Why do you love whom you love, and how long will it last? Do you know exactly what you are going to say before you say it? Why are you thinking your specific thoughts right now, and what will be your very next action? The weather is easier to predict than what you will be thinking, feeling, and doing next week—or even in ten seconds.

No matter how much you try to change, your life continues to unfold mysteriously, shaped by influences far beyond your control. Stuff happens, sometimes good, sometimes bad. In any case, as you get older, you feel something missing. Perhaps you don't care any more, and you settle into your life as good or bad as it is. But if you continue to grow, then you naturally become less interested in changing the patterns of your life and more devoted to opening and giving your deepest gifts of love, right now.

Change the things you can and accept the things you can't—and eventually open to feel deeper than the things you can and can't change. With practice, you can open and offer your deepest gifts regardless of how things are.

How do you open deeper? Opening is easier to do than to describe. Where is deep? Where do you feel hunches? Where do you feel your intuition? Where do you open when you love someone deeply—what part of you opens?

Your deepest gifts of love unfold from depth, spontaneously. Love's deep openness is your source of true change.

Suppose you were trying to tell your lover of your love for him or her. You could memorize a speech and say it word for word. Or, you could write down your feelings and read them to your lover. Both of these speeches might convey the right words, but your efforts may feel somewhat contrived.

If you were face to face with your lover right now, you could try speaking straight from your heart, without memorization or reading. How freely would your love flow from your heart into words? That depends, in part, on how open your body is. With tight lips, tight fists, and tight belly, your words may be true but their tone would be squinshed. To offer your true openness as love, now and in every moment you can practice to open your body.

From your heart, feel your jaw muscles, and let go of any unnecessary tension. Unfist your hands so your palms are open to the air. Unclench your belly so your entire body swells with breath. Breathe and relax open. An open body is not limp, but is like a cat, responsive, alive, and expressive.

Your open body is more able to conduct love without obstruction. Your words of love can flow from your heart to your lover without getting trapped in a cage of tension. An open body allows your depth to emerge more easily through your breath, words, and gestures.

To allow a deeper openness to prevail, feel into your lover's depth as if using feeling-sonar to touch far into your lover's heart. Breathe with your lover, relax open with your lover, open to heart-depth with your lover, and allow your words to flow.

Feel your lover's heart opening and closing as you speak, using your words like music to bring a smile to your lover's heart, gently evoking an openness of deep trust. Your lover can feel your depth feeling their depth, and so relax open with you. Allow your poetry to spring from open depth felt as one by both your hearts.

Your spontaneous heart-deep words often convey your true love with more grace and profundity than your rehearsed attempts to speak. This is so for all the patterns of your life.

For instance, if you are trying to change the patterns of your diet without feeling deeper, your changes will probably be superficial and clumsy. Many of your eating patterns are based on stress, loneliness, and hurt, as well as routines dictated by your schedule. When you feel deeper, then deeper expressions of love can emerge through your life—and through your style of eating.

Imagine that your lover has jilted you, and now you find yourself stuffing cookies in your mouth. First, locate any tension in your body. Feel the softness of your tongue, neck, and belly. Breathe and open your body.

Now feel deep into your heart, into the place where you feel deep love. Even if you don't feel love right now, feel into the place where you *would* feel love. Open to feel your deep heart. When you can feel your deep heart, even if your are hurting, allow yourself to let down your defenses, to feel whatever you are feeling fully, with no resistance.

Breathe as you feel open. Hurt and open. Breathe and open. Be open as whatever you are feeling. Allow deep openness to emerge through your tongue, neck, and belly. Allow openness to pervade your body as you would allow music to move through you while dancing. Allow your body to be lived as openness, as the flow of deep love opening outward from your heart, through your belly, hands, feet, and mouth.

You might forget to open, start thinking about your lover who betrayed you, and automatically tighten your belly, scrunch your face, and put a cookie in your mouth. As soon as you can remember, feel into your depth of heart, open, breathe, and allow your heart's deep feeling to open out through your entire body, even as you chew your cookie.

As openness, you will chew differently. You will swallow differently. The tense edge of reactive emotion will soften in the openness pervading outward from your heart through your skin. Open your skin to feel outward into the room. From your heart, through your belly, toes, hands, tongue, and face, feel outward, as if you were the space in the room, and beyond. Offer yourself as openness to all.

Practice this opening while your emotional patterns of hurt and your tense patterns of eating attempt to reassert themselves.

If you want to change the way you eat, practice opening, even while your eating patterns continue. Allow new patterns to emerge, spontaneously, moment by moment, from the openness of your depth. Practice opening with great discipline and allow your life-patterns to emerge spontaneously, from depth, as an open offering of love to all.

If you persist in this practice of deepening, your superficial patterns of thought, emotion, and action will be replaced by deeper, more loving, more gifting patterns. In any moment you lose your depth, your old habits reassert themselves. Even so, the practice isn't to fight against the old patterns of eating, but to feel more deeply and then open *as* that depth, from your heart, through your entire body, and outward to all.

If you are not living the life-habits you deeply want to, it may be because you are not yet opening consistently and allowing your deep heart to emerge through your body, moment by moment. Practice feeling, opening, and offering openness outward in every moment, breath by breath. Then, your life unfolds with grace and force, spontaneously patterned by the profound mystery opening out from your depth.

12

OPEN WHILE FAILING

∾⧢∾

No matter how hard you try,
your potential gifts are greater
than what you actually
give in your life.

At depth, you are infinite. If you allow yourself to feel who you are fully in this moment, you will find no horizon, no end. Everything you experience and do in your life is like a ripple on the surface of a boundless openness who you are.

At your heart, you can feel your depth open as love. Deep down, you know that you are *immense*. Sizeless, really, and of ultimate importance, or so it seems. Yet, if you look at your daily life, you find paltry enjoyments and picayune dramas.

You feel that your life can be truly significant, potentially full of love and great gifts. But it isn't playing out that way. It always feels less than you sense it can be. Your career isn't quite *it*, your intimate life isn't what it could be, your heart doesn't wholly love, and your mind can't sufficiently articulate your profundity. Your life may feel really good, but still, there is a depth of love and knowing that isn't quite making its way to your daily surface.

You can absorb yourself in family frolic, delicious meals, an interesting job, and great friends. Even when an unlived depth tickles your surface, there is always a phone call to make, a child who needs help, or something on TV. You don't have to pay attention to the unquenched callings from your deep heart. It's more comfortable to relish the tenderness between you and your loved ones, or the adventures of your daily routine. Your unlived depth can wait.

After all, even when you have *tried* to live from your depth, you have failed. Like an artist striving to capture deep vision on thin canvas, your masterpiece moments are few. Usually, no matter how skillfully you apply yourself day to day, your profession, sexual life, and spiritual reach fall short of the love and virtue you know is possible. Rather than churn in the constant friction of failure's abrasion, you may choose to glide in the goodness of so-far success: decent health, financial comfort, a home full of affection and care.

Still, in quiet moments of no distraction, you wonder. Your depth knows love without bounds, yet your relationships seem cleaved by membranes of mistrust. Your depth resonates with truth absolute, yet your expressions are somewhat stumped by fear. However beautiful your life seems, it is a tad more tawdry than your heart's grace would have it.

This is how it must be, and always is. The truth is that your daily life is but a thin strip of experience barely seeming in the profundity of who you are at depth. Your activities and relationships never capture the grandeur that wants to unfold from your heart into the world. There may be moments of palpable glory, brief openings through which magnificence effulges without curtail, but mainly your life is a tragic almost-there of unfulfilled longing and partial gestures of tense effort.

For the most part, your happiness is a sparse lie. You are deeper than your life shows, and you know it. You are more loving than your relationships allow, more brilliant than your career suggests. In your secret depth of being, you are infinite, creative, and boundless—and utterly unable to press your full glory into the world. So you settle for some comfort and assuage your lack with entertainments and, perhaps, unconsummated spiritual pursuits.

You are suffering depth's inability to effuse the world with boundless love and truth, with *your* boundless love and truth. If you allow yourself to feel this suffering, even amidst life's goodness, then your heart can open beyond delusion.

When you no longer need to distract yourself in affection and comfort, then you can enjoy your family's love and your career's adventure without lying to yourself that it is enough. It isn't.

Only depth is enough. Through real practice, you can feel open as the depth that you are, rather than remain mollified in goodness or depressed in futility. Life is good, and it is futile, and depth is true in any case. You can open as infinity even though your relationships and actions fall short. To collapse in failure—or to gloat in satisfaction—is to avoid opening as depth.

You can open as love and live as love, even though you are not fully received by those you love. You can open as infinity and offer your deepest truth, even though your gifts may be refused by those you want to serve. You can live as openness even though your daily life may seem tawdry in light of your heart's deepest shine.

You are not here to transform the world and create love on earth. In truth, you aren't here. Here is in you. You are openness. Abide as openness, live as love, and appear as limits. You really have no choice.

13

APPRECIATE
DISSATISFACTION

〜

*Dissatisfaction can
remind you to
open fully, now.*

Close your eyes for a moment, relax, and remember how it feels to be deep in sleep. Imagine, right now, that you are sound asleep. Let go of the world for a moment, and just rest in the place of sleep. With your eyes closed, sink into the deep bliss of sleep for a few minutes, without actually falling asleep.

Then slowly open your eyes, but continue to feel the bliss of sleep. Allow the world around you to appear, but stay in contact with the deep bliss of sleep. You can actually feel the deeply fulfilling quiet bliss of sleep even now, while you are awake. You can see the world around you and interact with people while maintaining feeling-connection with the part of you that is bliss-full of sleep, even now.

Practice to feel the bliss of sleep now and randomly throughout the day. Close your eyes briefly or leave them open, and for a moment fall into sleep's bliss. Feeling sleep's bliss, open your eyes and live your day, open to the world around you, while also remaining open to the ever-present bliss of sleep.

Right now, you can open to the world around you, as well as to your thoughts and emotions, and also to the silent purr, the blissful unseen fullness of sleep. Alternatively, you can limit yourself to just one part of who you are.

For instance, you can concentrate on your thoughts or get lost in your emotions, thus becoming unaware of the world around you, stubbing your toe. You may be drawn so fully into the world—running from one chore to another—that you lose touch with the ever-present bliss of sleep, thus feeling bereft of deep peace. You can also fall asleep and totally lose awareness of your thoughts and the world around you, while the water boils on the stove and you miss your appointment.

In any moment, you can limit yourself to one part of the open moment that is available to you, or you can practice to open and feel all with less bounds. Now and any time, you can open and feel your outer world of sight and sound, your inner world of thoughts and emotions, and also the deep, seamless, fullness of sleep's ever-present bliss. You can feel open as the entire moment, and then open as feeling itself, feeling open without *any* bounds, even as daily life continues.

Practice relaxing fully open, feeling all, for a few moments. Feel the bliss of deep sleep right now, and also continue with your thoughts while your eyes are open to the light of day. As you practice opening—feeling from unseen depth through inner world to the vivid light that is your day—your hold on "who you are" relaxes. You are a character that moves through your world all day, but also you are a character in your daydreams and nightdreams, as well as being the unbodied bliss-fullness of deep sleep.

You are openness, enjoying the undisturbed depth of sleep's bliss as well as the everyday adventures of inner and outer life. And right now, you can open as all of you, from blissful depth to agitated surface.

You become unhappy in any moment that you assume you are limited to the surface, to the body of daily adventure. You feel partial. You can intuit deep openness—full of love and light, utterly free of constraint—but you can't seem to find and keep it in your life.

So you search for deeper love in your relationships and more freedom in your lifestyle, but it never adds up to the open fullness that you secretly know is your true home. You try to arrange yourself and the world so your suffering diminishes, but always there is the continual stress of hoping for more success or love.

You cannot arrange yourself or the world in order to experience openness, but in any moment you can simply feel open.

Everything in this world dies. No arrangement lasts. Your fancy car will get scratched, your body will become diseased, your lover will betray you or vanish. Dissatisfaction is healthy; you are sensitive to the truth—you are suffering as things change and disappear.

The more profound truth is that you are alive as unbound love-fullness, deep as sleep, wide as awake. In the roll of everything happening, feel open as this entire moment, just as it is, as deep as you are.

Relax open your belly. Ease open your mind. Feel open where sleep's bliss abides. Feel your thoughts and emotions and perceptions bloom open and gone. Breathe the openness of the moment in and out of your heart, as if you were breathing the changing colors of the day, inhaling and exhaling the light of a dream, breathing the bliss of deep sleep, in and out, breathing the love that lives as everyone, in and out, as you melt full open feeling all.

Welcome dissatisfaction as a reminder, and practice feeling open as this entire moment. Open, now and ever, allowing your actions to blossom as love.

14

DON'T WAIT
FOR PERFECTION

~∞~

*You can be
wide open and
diseased at the
same time.*

No matter how sick you are in body or mind, you can still open. Disease may ravage your body and drugs may cloud your mind, and you can still open. Deep openness can encompass *all* states of body and mind.

Physical and psychological disorders need not obscure your openness, and your openness may not affect your pathologies. If you inherited nearsightedness from your parents, then spiritual openness probably won't change your need to wear glasses. If your mind has adapted to habits of panic instilled by years of childhood abuse, then spiritual openness probably won't eliminate your cringe at the sight of your lover's genitals.

However, you can be a myopic neurotic and still open with the freedom of unbound love. You may squint and become nauseated as your lover disrobes, but the humor of your response can avail. Like a muscular tic or a snotty nose, your emotional responses are natural effects of your history—perhaps uncomfortable, running their course largely beyond your immediate control. Nevertheless, you can offer your love, laughter, and openness even as you sniffle, panic, or shriek.

Right now, unique as you are in body and mind, you can practice opening fully.

Even as you open, laugh, and love, the patterns of your body and mind have their own momentum. Heart disease, cancer, and even alcoholism have continued in the disposition of many deeply open men and women. Every kind of sexual style and twist can be found in the biographies of saints and spiritual teachers. Your openness can be real and profound, and still your bodymind ripples on, patterning itself according to past influence and present habit.

If your mother drank too much alcohol or was in a state of constant emotional stress during her pregnancy, then your nervous system is somewhat shaped by the chemicals that coursed through your embryonic growth, and there isn't much you can do about that now. As a consequence of your mother's actions, your body may be small, your mental acuity may be weak, and your emotional flow may be unstable. These are simply some of the patterns that you may feel and learn to open as, moment by moment.

If your father sexually molested you, then now as an adult you may react to your lover's advances with numbness. Your posture may be hunched and your pelvis locked. The patterning of your bodymind is what it is. You can change it to some degree, but you can always open as it is, even now. Open now, offering your heart's gift, and also do your best to live rightly through the present patterns of your past history.

Have you ever done something you wished you had done differently? If so, you can learn from your mistakes and try to do better next time. If the patterns of your bodymind cause undue suffering, in your life or in the lives of others, you can work to transform these patterns, heal them as much as possible, and grow more fully into a balanced, integrated, and healthy person.

But this growth is not the same as spiritual openness and depth. A balanced, healthy individual may serve to create positive changes in the world and yet be unwilling to open and feel fully. On the other hand, someone may be wide open and feeling all, yet appear to be a raving lunatic, lustful, and drug-addicted. Such a person may, in fact, be crazy, lustful, and drug-addicted—and yet be open so deeply their heart feels more than you can know and their love extends to you without bounds.

No matter how fully you open and live as love, your character is only slightly changeable. Your pre-birth influences are ingrained in your nervous system like rings in a tree. Childhood stresses still waltz in the chemistry of your brain and emotions. Even the evolutionary travails of your furry mammalian ancestors contribute to your so-called "spontaneous" desires for sex, food, and comfort.

You are birthed by, grown within, and taken apart by an immense and mysterious web of influence. The efforts you make to be healthy and helpful can be nullified by a falling rock caused by a sudden earth tremor or by a heart failure predisposed by the genetics of your father's mother's father. You may truly want to serve your 16-year-old daughter's friend, and yet you can't seem to shake the sexual desire you feel, or the guilt.

Integrity is well worth a lifetime of cultivation. Serving others is really the only way to live your heart's truth. But you are not cured thereby.

Your body may remain bent and your mind may remain twisted. Still, love can extend through your distortions, uniquely twisted yet unbound. Great gifts of openness, love, and awakening can be given—*have* been given—through arthritic fingers and alcohol-drenched brain cells.

Even as lust, greed, and anger continue to arise in your emotional patterns formed by years of mammalian struggle, parental abuse, and self-torture, you can practice opening without bounds. You can practice opening and giving your deepest gifts in every present moment, however awry your body and mind—and the world—remain.

Feel whatever love you can in this moment, however small. Even if you are woozily soused or ravenous with lust, find a kernel of openness deep in your heart. Feel the place in you that wants to give love and be fully received in love, no matter how messed up you are. Locate your desire for love, for openness, for freedom, even if it is tiny. In the midst of your drunken stupor or wild ire, reconnect with this speck of openness.

Breathe in and out of this tiny gist of love, while you open your senses and feel the people and place around you. Even if you can only open a little bit to breathe through your heart and feel the people and world around you, this is a little bit more open than staying closed.

Practice opening a tiny amount while your body and mind reel on, numb, confused, spinning. Breathe love in and out of the feeling-space of your heart. Breathe the force of love deep down into your abdomen, opening the closures in your gut by inhaling full and filling your belly round. Feel the heart of those around you, look into their eyes, open your senses to all the world's display, and offer your full-bellied love through your twists by degrees, in every moment you can remember to practice opening.

As slurred as your speaking may be, offer words of love. Through your shaking hands, offer openness through your service. Feel the hearts of those around you as they open or close in response to your gifts. As dim as your awareness may be fuddled, practice to feel the hearts around you and act to open them. Don't wait for perfection—or even to get straight—to offer your deepest love, full-bellied and open hearted.

Offer your gifts right now with the deepest integrity you can through whatever kinks may remain, always feeling and breathing the hearts of others as you act. Do your best to heal yourself and others, remembering that habits and history may budge very little. Nevertheless, this present moment comes and goes open, just as it is.

15

Do Love
Through Your Body

Feeling who you are
is the first step;
living true to your
identity is next.

⟨⟩

Your identity is who you feel you are. If you feel you are a corporate executive, you will act very differently than if you feel you are infinite light. Who you feel yourself *as* is your identity. Spiritual growth involves deepening your identity, feeling more deeply who you are.

But after you have discovered a certain level of depth, then you must conform your thoughts, emotions, and behaviors to this depth of openness—otherwise, your life-practice lags behind your identity-practice. Suppose, for example, you realize that at heart you are love. You realize that although you might function as a mother, a politician, or a baker, at depth you actually *are* love.

This realization is half of your spiritual practice. The other half is to live true to your newly realized identity, *in spite of old habits to the contrary.* You can now practice to *do* love. When you walk, how can you let go of your old habits of tension and move as an expression of the love you feel you are at depth? At your job, how can you work as the love you truly are? What changes do you need to make in your daily life-rituals so that love can radiate through your every breath, action, and relationship?

Most people find it much easier to grow deeper in identity ("Who am I?") than to express this depth through daily life. They discover they are love, for instance, and still spend hours gossiping or watching TV. They self-justify by thinking they can be love while also lazing around, and this is true. But if they were really sensitive and honest with themselves, they would feel that certain behaviors conduct love more than others do. Singing with a relaxed throat is more conducive to expressing love than singing with a tense throat, although you can love and also be tense. You can make love with a hard belly or a soft belly, but love flows more fully through a soft belly.

"Am I receiving love from others fully into my body? Is love flowing through my body outward to others fully?" You learn to feel the flow of love as feedback. Before, you were able to bad-mouth others with a laugh and a sneer. Now that you have opened more deeply, you can feel how such gossip creates a subtle closure, a tension in yourself and in the friends you are speaking with. So you practice living more true to the depth of love you are, which in this case may mean gossiping less so love can flow more fully through your body and your friends.

You can notice how your diet affects the openness in yourself and others. True, you can be open as love and eat anything. Nevertheless, certain foods may contribute to a subtle closure in your body, emotions, and mind, and therefore instigate closure in your relationships.

Love, or openness, is. You can practice opening just as you are. As you grow in your capacity to *be* openness, you can also grow in your capacity to *do* openness. Your body, mind, and actions—whether in dreams or while awake—can live more or less true to the love-openness that is their source.

Whatever appears in any moment, including right now—your thoughts, the room, other people—is the given medium for love's emergence. You don't have much control over *what* appears, but you can practice true to your realized depth—or not. You can choose to gift the world and all others with the deepest love or openness that you can open as. You can practice to think as openness, to act as openness, to breathe as openness, now and in any moment. You can feel the texture of every moment of every relationship and act to align your words and touch and gaze so the openness of love prevails.

You can practice living as the deepest openness that you know you are. One enemy of this practice is laziness, or the misconception that *knowing* you are love is sufficient. Knowing or feeling the deep openness who you are is fairly easy; *living* as this openness, and *serving* all others to live as this love, in every moment through all appearances, is where the art is.

Usually, there is substantial lag time between the realization of depth and your capacity to live it. Your emotions, sex, and relationships tend to be much less open than who you feel you are at depth. True art requires practice. Living as an artful expression of openness—so even the tone of your voice, the grace of your gestures, and the play of your sexing are exquisite expressions of the love who you are—requires years of spontaneous gifting and rigorous practice.

If *knowing* the truth is sufficient for you, then practice the art of philosophy. If only *living* the truth will suffice, then practice the art of love through your mind, your emotions, and your body. Do your best to breathe love, in and out.

Receive the presence of the entire moment deep into your body—into your heart, into your belly, into your loins—as a lover would open deeply to receive her trusted beloved. *Give* your deepest love, pressing your love into the moment's openness without holding anything back, as a lover would press his love gently and deeply into his trusting beloved. Soften your belly as love. Speak so that listeners open. Prepare food and arrange your house as love's radiant gifts of enchantment.

Even in your nighttime dreams, your daydreams, and your secret moments of private time, practice the art of *doing* love through whatever medium appears. When you notice your mind wandering to a sexual fantasy, consciously guide the imagery toward love's fullness, so that all the characters in the fantasy are heartfully served by your sexual gifts and opened as love's unbound ecstasy.

If you find yourself lonely, raiding the refrigerator at night, suck the fullness of the moment deep into your heart with each swallow, and allow each mouthful's joy to radiate outward, breathing your secret pleasure as a gift freely offered from your heart through your whole body to all.

In this way, every place that comes and goes also opens as love fully offered.

16

Be Reminded
by Jealousy

❧

*Jealousy points
to your false
hopes of fulfillment.*

If you think money will make you happy, then you will be jealous of
wealthy people. If you think sex will fulfill you, then you will be jealous
of passionate lovers. Whenever you believe that something or someone,
some insight or some experience will truly make you happy, you are
wrong. Only opening as you *are* is true happiness. You suffer jealousy
when you forget this.

Jealousy is the sting of false hope. Even when you get that for which you
are jealous—a beautiful girlfriend, fame, a man who truly loves you, great success—nothing essential changes. You are open or closed, various experiences
come and go, everything gained is threatened by loss, and nothing is quite as
fulfilling as your jealousy promises.

Many people have less than you do. They are jealous of you. If they were
you, how blissful would they be right now?

Bliss is the nature of deep openness. Nothing other than openness—not
money, knowledge, or relationship—truly increases or decreases your bliss.

This is easy to understand. Still, you are probably jealous of certain people. You want what they have.

This feeling of jealousy is a useful sign. Feel it fully. Part of you hates them for having what you don't. Part of you justifies that you are better off without it. Part of you feels inferior for not having it. Part of you tries to feel superior by not needing it.

This complex wad of jealousy is a sign that you aren't relaxed as openness. If you are jealous of someone who seems to have a good intimate relationship, then you are refusing to open fully with the relationship (or lack of relationship) that you *do* have. You still hope for something more. You still are requiring a change of relationship before you are willing to surrender wide open as love.

This sense of waiting, as if the future might offer you something more fulfilling than this moment, is the essence of jealous suffering. Your heart and body clench with stress as you refuse to open now. Jealousy is a sign that you are waiting.

Suppose you are jealous because your friend has five million dollars in the bank. Feel your jealousy with precision. Is it hot or cold? Red or black? Sharp or dull? Do you feel jealous in your belly or heart? Feel every sensation, and also feel the emotional roots of your sensations.

The knot in your gut, for instance, is probably rooted in your feeling of insufficiency. You are waiting for a future event—having more money—to make you feel sufficiently secure to open. You are waiting, actively refusing to open as unbound consciousness and love right now. You believe that if you only had what your friend has—more money—*then* the moment would be sufficient, and you would be able to relax open.

The truth is that you can open as every moment, exactly as painful or pleasurable as it is. You are open as the entire moment now or to some degree closing—unwilling to feelingly breathe *all* into your deep heart and offer *all* wide open to infinity—therefore suffering your tension, waiting for future fulfillment or release.

You may need to follow in your friend's footsteps, acquire riches, and surround yourself in the image of your relief. Then, sitting in the midst of your acquisitions, the evidence will be incontrovertible: Something still feels missing. Still, you are jealous of someone or something. Still waiting.

While you are unwilling to open as you are, jealousy reminds you of what you are waiting for. Keep searching for that thing until the search is exhausted, until your life feels meaningless, until you have tried and tried and you still feel unfulfilled by what you have or haven't acquired.

Whenever you are ready, this moment is sufficient. You can open deeply right now. Your relief, your fulfillment in any moment, is as unbounded as your openness.

In moments of envy, seethe in the pang of jealousy without consolation. Be jealous fully, without closing. Open wide as possible even while squirming as jealousy. Breathe the entire moment in and out of your jealous heart. Allow the moment's presence to penetrate into your deepest heart, and allow your heart to give love outward without limit, feeling out beyond all you can sense or know. As jealousy wide open, look into your friend's eyes and see that his openness is the same openness you are.

Your life is adorned with various gains and losses, pleasures and pains. In the midst of every present moment, you are either opening or closing. You are either feeling all while giving your deepest gifts of love or you are waiting.

Jealousy is the stress of being reminded that you are waiting.

17

EXPRESS WHO
YOU REALLY ARE

⁓

*Every desire reveals
your true nature.*

Every day you want to do many things, from hugging your lover to earning money. Why? What feeling underlies all your hopes and dreams? This feeling is the tension between who you *really* are and who you *assume* yourself to be.

Consider your desire for intimate relationship. There are many reasons for engaging in a relationship. But you only feel utterly fulfilled in intimacy when you and your lover trust each other so much that you are willing to let down your guards, open your hearts, and love. This is your deepest desire in intimacy because, in truth, you *are* open as love—but you assume yourself to be a separate, isolated individual. So you scheme and dream to experience in your relationship what, in truth, you already are.

You want to enjoy financial security because, in truth, you *are* abundance, although you assume only effort will provide a feeling of ease. You enjoy dangerous sports because in every moment you *are* at the edge of death—the ultimate edge of winning or losing—and yet your assumed security makes you seek risks. You want to eat chocolate because, deep in your heart, you *are* blissful fullness, though you often close to its pleasure and so seek its taste.

Through your daily round, you seek to approximate the truth of who you *are* that you have lost touch with. This drama of approximation is the story of your life. You never quite succeed like you hope to. You never quite get the love you really want. And so you either try harder or give up trying. In either case, you are missing the point of existence.

The open expression of who you really are is the only thing that will free you from the stress of feeling incomplete. In truth, you *are* what you want.

The farther you wander from who you truly are, the more you crave the qualities you miss. Since you can't feel the love that lives you, you look to your lover to cherish you. Divorced from your home of unlimited openness, you seek to expand the sphere of your power, the size of your portfolio, the borders of your country. Desiring the freedom of inherent ease, you try to discharge stress through masturbation, conversation, and secret habits of release. You miss the simplicity of being, so you seek it in the warmth of a heroin rush, a fluffy bed, or a ritual cup of coffee.

At times, you fret over your appearance, seeking to find the radiance you truly are. You think to yourself constantly, providing a reflection of your own presence. Yet, in truth, you *are* utter presence, whether or not you reflect yourself by thinking.

Whenever you are ready, you can stop trying to find what you are precluding and start being who you are in truth. To surrender so completely to be who you are is terrifying—your self-image instantly vanishes. Yet it is the only way to live that is real. Otherwise, in every moment of missing who you truly are, you create a self-image that isn't the real thing. You feel a lack. This tension of deficiency can wind into an intense twist of desire. Eventually, you can become quite warped.

Craving the depth that you miss, you may find yourself engaging in crime, lying, self-abuse, and terrorizing others—or perhaps just sitting in front of the TV and eating cookies. No matter how extreme or mediocre your misplaced efforts become, you can always open as your source. In the midst of stealing, for instance, you can open as the abundance of life-force that you *are*. How will you act as abundant fullness? Open as you are, your twist unwinds.

In your most wound-up, naughty moments of sicko indulgence, as well as in your common round of daily drudge, you are only missing who you truly are. Through years of moment-by-moment practice, you can open as every twist and hope. You can live open as love, alive as spontaneous blessing.

What you want is who you are. Open as you are without hesitation.

18

LIVE AS LOVE

∾

First you are selfish,
then you try to help others,
then you open and live as love.

In young adulthood, you are mostly concerned about yourself. You want to
live comfortably, work at a decent job, enjoy a good intimate relationship,
perhaps start a family. Some years pass and you may begin to feel wider. Your
attention literally expands beyond your personal life and family to encompass
the lives of others. You feel moved to help others in some way.

You don't *stop* being concerned with your personal and family life. It's just
that now you *also* begin to include more people in your scope of concern.
You might volunteer or donate money to help others. You might coach a little
league team or work to reduce international hunger. You have grown free
enough from concerns about your personal life so that you naturally want to
offer some of your surplus energy to others.

Eventually, though, if you really get into helping others, you may start
to despair. After years of working to serve others, you begin to burn out.
The resistance to your love seems relentless. You give and give and so what?
Sometimes it seems that people don't even want to grow or learn to help

themselves. Your attempt to help others, even your own children, often creates further problems that you can't foresee. After years of enthusiastic service you begin to notice you are getting tired and people are stuck in the same old patterns and the world continues to churn like a big machine of virtually imperturbable momentum.

This is an accurate perception. The world is much larger than your person. Individuals rarely make full use of the help they are offered. Even the most selfless, loving, and powerful people in the history of humanity—religious and political visionaries, for instance—have barely made a dent in the strife of the world, and have often initiated movements that inadvertently resulted in immeasurable death and destruction.

Once you grow wider than your personal self, the relentless suffering in the world can move you to grow deeper. You can eventually realize that whether or not this world gets better, your purpose is to open as love. Your children may hate you, lakes and oceans may become irrevocably poisoned, the earth and every person on it may be a temporary flash in cosmic history. Even so, openness is. The only true way to live is open. To collapse in despair—or to inflate yourself with hope—is to separate yourself from open depth.

Every moment is unbound and free. Every experience and perception magically appears and disappears without a trace. You are the openness that is the indisputable truth of every moment. Eventually, practicing to open as this truth is the only way to live.

Throughout your life, whenever you close, you suffer. And then you go through the same basic sequence of concerns. At first, your concern is limited to your personal comfort, relationships, and achievements. Then your life begins to feel small, so you enlarge your scope of concern. You offer your energy to serve others. Eventually, your efforts to help others and better the planet feel trivial in the face of the world's chug-a-lug immensity. At this point, you either retreat back to your personal cave of small comforts or continue to serve others as you fight burn-out and convince yourself that you are doing the "right thing." Or, you realize each moment's openness.

Even when you are stopped dead in your tracks in your efforts to give love—perhaps the recipient of your help spits in your face or the government blocks your altruistic labors—the moment is still wide open. No edges hedge this moment. No boundaries limit your opening as love. Even when you feel frustrated, angry, or defeated, the indisputable truth is that this moment, including you, is open without bounds. You *are* infinity, briefly texturing as frustration, anger, or the feeling of defeat.

You are free when you open as this moment, fully feeling the very real textures of pain and pleasure, inhaling the entire moment including you and all others deep into your heart, feeling outward and offering yourself as the entire moment open without bounds. When you act as this openness while feeling all, love is expressed through everything you do. Love is offered without expecting returns. You are alive *as* love. All beings benefit from your openness, and your life is an offering of spontaneous gifting, in every situation, even as the world crumbles or lasts a few more years.

19

REMAIN OPEN
WHEN DISGUSTED

∽

*Everyone is
as you are.*

Relax open as you are, right now. Be willing to feel everything. Allow the moment to come and go freely as you relax open. The entire moment, including you, shines as light, feels as love, and is intensely present as open consciousness. You are open without limit, as every part of you and the world show and go wide open.

Everyone is this same boundless openness, although anyone may act to close and feel separate. Whenever you do the act of separating from an other, then your heart and theirs suffer, and you create suffering in the world around you.

At heart, you are openness, as is everyone. The idiot on TV that you find so disgusting is the same openness that you are. The rapist you despise is as you are. The foreign dictator you abhor is as you are. To pull away from someone, to feel different at heart, is to enact a lie of separation.

Everyone that you hate, from your mother-in-law to a serial murderer, is, at heart, you. Closing your heart to theirs means pinching away from who you are. This act of pinching creates the sense of inner stress and unfinished yearning that most people suffer. Every moment that you enact the lie of difference, you reinforce distress in your heart.

Certainly, some people are disgusting. At times, everyone is. If people could see all of you, inside and out, they would see radiant beauty and repugnant ugliness. You might not act out your inner twists as loudly as the cretin on TV, but you are surely twisted. There are moments when you even disgust yourself.

Disgust, nausea, loathing—some aspects of yourself and others surely deserve such abhorrent gut responses. But disgust doesn't create suffering—recoil does. Separation is the act of unlove.

To grow spiritually, to deepen the openness of your heart, you can practice being disgusted without pulling away. You can learn to become nauseated without closing down. The truth is, *pulling back in separation* is the source of deep suffering in you and others. If you can stay open and feel everyone fully, even those who actively disgust you, then love endures.

Disgust may be your natural response to some people all the time and to everyone sometime. But closing down and pulling away is an additional act of unlove that creates suffering in you and the world. Your *separation* is the deed of unlove, not your loathing or judgment.

You can try not to judge others, but even that is based on a judgment: "People who are non-judgmental are better than people who judge." The fact is, feeling good or bad in response to others is natural and inevitable. The trouble starts when you allow your emotional response and mental judgments to result in heart-closure and separation. When you clench your belly, close your heart, and pull away from others, then you are actively creating unlove and suffering. It's one thing to be disgusted by some jerk; it's another thing to close your heart and add separation.

You can be open as love even when someone is acting in the vilest way. If necessary, you can move against an adversary with great force, and still you can remain open, feeling your opponent's heart as if it were yours or your lover's.

Again, when you pull back in closure, you create the distress of ongoing separation and perpetuate the anguish of unlove. Your disgust and loathing are natural emotional responses; separating your feeling heart, pulling away from those who disgust you, is the additional act of unlove, the original moment of deep suffering.

When you look into the eyes of those who most disturb you, practice feeling the openness behind the face of their fear and distress. Whether they are on TV or standing in front of you, no matter how closed or twisted they may be acting, feel through their pained expressions into their yearning heart. Their moment is open as yours, though they may be closing, unwilling to open as love, and therefore they are suffering their denial of love's openness.

Feel into their heart without adding your own closure or self-protection. Breathe openly with their heart as if breathing with a lover. Perhaps speak from your openness to their openness. If appropriate, touch or tussle to help loosen their cringe around love's open bloom. As uncomfortable as you may be, practice opening your body. Even if you are repulsed or furious, practice to keep your belly soft, your jaw relaxed, and your heart unclenched as you feel into their heart, open to open.

When someone disgusts you, and in every moment, practice to relax as the moment blooms open as every body. Allow openness the opportunity to live through you and your relationships by practicing to feel and breathe the deep openness that in everyone yearns to flower as love.

20

UNDO ALL EFFORT

෨ඬ

*In every moment
of real practice,
your effort undoes
the need for effort.*

Suppose you feel trapped by financial lack. You feel anxious. Your gut clenches. Your mind reels into a jumbled knot. You feel miserable. You don't know what to do.

First, you can feel exactly what you feel: the physical tightness, the mental racing, the emotional anguish. Breathe these textures of closure in and out of your heart. Then, feeling *as* these textures, heat them up. Actually feel your feelings becoming hot, and evaporating. For many people, it is easier to learn to open while heating the texture of their closure to evaporation. Eventually, you no longer need to heat up closure. You can simply feel fully, and as the feeling's texture, open.

As the feelings open, feel *as* the openness. Be openness, feeling openness.

Resting as openness, feel whatever you feel, as openness. Feel any remaining tension in your belly or thoughts in your head as textures of openness. As openness, examine your situation, make decisions about your career, and devise a plan of action to put your financial life back on track.

If you lose this openness as you plan to carry out your actions, then practice feeling your closure fully. Feel and breathe its texture. As the closure, heat it up and open as its texture, feeling whatever you feel as openness.

Eventually, this entire practice takes place instantaneously. You notice closure, and open. Openness abides—for a while. Again, you can notice closure, allow yourself to *be* closure, then, feeling as closure, heat it up and open.

You can practice opening in every moment. In truth, you *are* openness. This is why such practice is instantly and deeply effective: you are only *doing* what you *are*.

Practice is absolutely necessary, although you are only practicing what you *are*. Suffering is the felt difference between what you seem to feel and what you would be feeling if you allowed yourself to feel what actually *is*.

In other words, you are habitually *doing* a feeling of closure. When you practice to feel as openness, then the habit of closure is undone. In truth, you *are* openness, always. Even the entire moment of seeming closure is wide open, now and every now. Feeling as openness is simply feeling what is true, although you have habits to the contrary.

Suppose you are with your lover but you feel closed, separate, alone. You can practice to open. You can look into your lover's eyes and try to feel into your lover's heart. You can practice to connect heart to heart, so your love feels your lover's love, even through the closure-mood of the moment. You can allow your breath as one with your lover.

Breathing as one, feeling as one love, you are doing openness. In moments of real love, you know this is true—you *are* open as one. You and your lover want nothing more than to live as this truth, to live this truth through your bodies, to merge together and open as one, to feel *as* each other, alive as one love, even sexually.

This intuition of open oneness is at the root of your deep yearning. If you are dissatisfied with your love life, it is precisely because, deep down, you know how open love can be.

You and your lover may be afraid to be open, afraid of being hurt, afraid of opening without a story, without a future or past, without a drama or strategy for self-protection or self-worth. Yet you yearn to open as one love, and so this tension defines your life. The difference between your true openness and the closure you do creates the necessity for practice.

Practice, then, is simply to *do* what you truly *are*. In any moment of effective practice, the need for practice is alleviated. You realize that you *are* what you were trying to achieve or create. You are openness, alive as love.

Every moment is a cusp. If you abide as openness, then what *is* also seems to be. If you miss this mark even slightly, you slide down the slope into apparent problems. Love seems to be separation. Openness seems to be closure. Spontaneity seems to be effort. And yet, all the while, opening as what *is* instantaneously reveals the truth.

You *are* what *is* right now, you are the openness of love right now, even if your lover is screwing your best friend. Practice abiding open as the cusp of this moment without clinging to a single experience for a millisecond, lest you initiate a vortex of clench. This practice of abiding open as the form of every experience—opening *as* the texture of jealousy, opening *as* the texture of anger, opening *as* the texture of deciding to get a divorce—this practice can be lived naturally, loosely, yet relentlessly.

Opening as the cusp of this moment, all is as it is, wide open. Clenched as the vortex of clinging, grabbing onto that, pushing away from this, openness is forgotten in the swirl of edges. Your lover did this to you, so you are going to do that back. Your bank account is low so your gut contracts and fear motivates your career choices.

From the vortex of clench, all thoughts and actions beget further clench. Open as the cusp of this moment, all thoughts and actions emerge from depth and open without a trace. As you are. As this moment is.

Practice undoes itself open.

LOVE & SEX

21

ALLOW LOVE'S HURT

⁓

Opening your heart to love
also opens your heart to hurt.

Love is openness. When you allow yourself to open, then love can flow unimpeded. When your heart is open, you can commune with your lover, or anyone else. You can open with them in oneness. Whether you are having sex or discussing politics, you can open and commune as one love expressing itself through two bodies.

When you are open and the other is not, you will feel it. When your lover lashes out at you with vicious criticism, your heart feels slashed and wounded.

Eventually, your heart closes in order to feel less vulnerable. Yet you still desire love. Behind your walls of protection, your yearning backs up into frustration and then anger. Filling with rage, you may finally strike out at your lover, trying to hurt the one who has hurt you. You both close even more. You want their love and they won't give it to you, so you punish your lover for not loving you, and then he or she closes down more and punishes you back.

To break this cycle of closure, you can learn to practice love. You can practice remaining open even when your heart reflexively wants to close in order to guard itself from hurt. You can choose to feel the hurt and practice to stay open. Instead of closing in anger, allow yourself to feel your deep sorrow, your raw yearning, the wounding slashes of your lover's anger, and practice opening. By staying open, the cycle is broken, and your love awaits your lover's readiness to open.

In response to your lover's hurtful words and actions, you can practice love. Instead of holding your breath, you can breathe deeply and fully. Instead of tensing your body, you can relax your belly while you breathe and feel deep hurt. Instead of turning away, you can look into your lover's eyes while you feel their pain. You can serve your lover's openness by offering yours.

Feel into your lover's heart, beating yearningly, waiting for love behind their unloving guard. Rather than reacting to unlove by closing down, you can remain open and deeply connected, breathing and feeling the deep heart openness which hides behind the hurt of your lover.

You can practice this openness and deep heart-contact with everyone you love—in fact, with everyone. Whoever you are with, look into their eyes. Feel through their mask or social face, and feel into their heart's desire; they want to open, to connect and feel deep love, just like you do.

With whomever you choose, feel through their layers of habitual guardedness, their muscular tension, their lonely closure and protection. Without actually touching them, you can allow your heart to feel theirs. Inhale and exhale love with them as if doing heart-to-heart resuscitation from a distance. All of this can take place in a fraction of a second, casually, even with a grocery store clerk who remains unaware of any practice on your part.

Life is a lesson of love. Your life feels full in every moment you stay open as love, however painful or joyous the love is. If you close, even for a moment, then you are creating unfulfillment in your heart and pain in the heart of those who would open in love with you.

For your life to feel profound and full of love's power, practice opening at all times, including times of hurt. Feel and breathe your heart's deep hurt, and the hurt of others, without closing. Offer the openness of your heart to everyone, and especially to those who are wounding you. The only alternative is to close and live unfulfilled.

22

RECOGNIZE
YOUR REFUSAL

❧

Unless you are opening,
everything you do, think,
and feel is actively
refusing openness.

You want so badly to be accepted as you are. You want to feel worthy, acknowledged, and loved. These desires to be seen and felt as worthy are symptoms of your closure. The self-reflexive tension you call "me" is trying to sustain itself. Your emotional sustenance is grounded in this need to be mirrored, to know that you are seen, felt, and loved.

In truth, in depth, you *are* the openness of love. But as a separate "me," you are the refusal of this openness. You are the tension of self-sustenance, fidgeting to touch yourself, masturbating, filling your mouth with food, thinking about yourself, self-concerned. Even your desire to grow spiritually is self-concern. Everything you do acts to sustain the felt sense that you are a separate self, hopefully on the road to greater love and freedom.

Sustaining your sense of separate self is the refusal of love. For most of every day, you are actively refusing to be the openness that is love. You would rather be a closed someone with a personal life of pain and pleasure than openness alive as all beings and things.

Blue Truth

There are two major phases in spiritual growth. During the first phase, you actually believe you want to grow more open. You believe that you want more love in your life, more caring. You want to give your love and help others. You believe that your thoughts, feelings, and actions can actually lead toward getting and giving more openness and love.

The second phase begins when you can feel, moment by moment, that you are actively closing. Every thought, feeling, and action is reinforcing your sense of separateness. You are *doing* unlove. In fact, "me" is the very act of unlove. "Me-ing" is the process of holding back, protecting yourself, hoping to be cherished, hoping to grow open, thinking to yourself, strategizing for your success. You are utterly self-involved. Everything you do is an effort to sustain this sense of me that is hopefully loved, loving, and successful.

When this second phase of life begins, you realize that you absolutely do not want to grow in openness. Truly, you are terrified of being open. You want to be a little bit open in order to feel comfortable and safe, but total openness—without any "me" you can point to—is terrifying.

In truth, you are love, not a "me" that wants to love and be loved. The me-ing that wants to be separate and loved may continue with momentum from the past, but you can treat this me-ing with the same care you would a bowel movement. It is something to be felt as it occurs, sometimes enjoyed, sometimes suffered, and naturally released, as time will have it.

If you want to obsess about the movement of "me," about your emotions, thoughts, and actions, about who loves you or whether your career or spiritual practice will succeed, you can do so for as long as you want. At some point, you realize that all this movement is natural, but it doesn't go anywhere profound.

Why be obsessed with your own do-do? When you reduce yourself to this process of me-ing, you are actively refusing to be the love who you are, open, boundless, and free.

23

LET LOVE
LIVE AS ANGER

∽

*You can be open in love
and also full of anger.*

Many people seem to believe that to love means to be sweet and peaceful. But love is openness. All emotional expressions are waves in an ocean of love. Even anger can move in deep love.

Imagine that you find your children at the open cabinet beneath your kitchen sink. Your daughter has a bottle of drain cleaner to her lips. Your son is about to pour bleach in his eyes. You baby girl is about to drink insecticide.

Without thinking, you shout, "No!" You grab the poisons away from your children and shout, "No, no, no! Don't play with these! They're dangerous!" You may even shake your children, squeezing their shoulders tightly. You shake them because you love them so much. Then you hold your crying children tightly to your chest. "I love you! I love you so much. I don't want you to hurt yourselves."

Because your anger comes from love, soon your body softens, your children stop crying, and they feel your care. Your eyes are as moist as your children's. They feel your love, but they also know the urgency of your demand: Danger! Your anger cuts through the casualness of the moment.

This is serious business. A quiet and gentle voice doesn't convey your love with the same urgency, power, and consequence.

As you grow in your capacity to stay open under all circumstances, your emotions become stronger, not weaker. If your husband is wasting his life, frittering away his time in trivial pursuits, distracted by TV and lost causes, your heart will shout its love: "I can't stand when you are like this! You are a great man! I want to feel your fullest gifts!" The urgency of your demand for his fullest potential is unmistakable.

If your wife is blabbing because she is tense, hardly looking in your eyes, prattling on in a superficial way, your heart may shout: "I love you! Enough of this! I want to feel you open with me!" Your sudden thunderbolt of love can crack her surface tension so for a moment she stops. You can swoop in while she is surprised, embracing her in openness, pervading her with your deep and present love.

Some people aren't ready for uninhibited love. If your lover is a person who has been abused in the past, he or she may need well-established boundaries in order to grow: You are allowed to say you're angry, but not to shout it. Or, you are allowed to shout your anger, but not to touch your lover angrily. Boundaries provide a sense of safety, which some people need in order to practice staying open and not be paralyzed by fear.

But as you grow, there comes a time when you and your lover are unwilling to settle for anything less than unrestrained love. You both want to give and receive unconfined, unsuppressed, untamed love. This kind of love may yell and scream and cry and demand—without warning—because your desire for openness and communion is so intense.

Everybody closes now and then. Everybody has his or her moments of laziness, superficiality, and mediocrity. Therefore, patience, kindness, and support are the essential matrix of a healthy relationship. But some moments require passion's intervention. As with your children drinking poison under the sink, your love's urgency won't allow your intimate relationship to wither and die. If you lover is threatening their own growth by being less open than he or she can be, then your loving heart is free to roar.

Love can be gentle and nurturing. But love can also be angry, when you are open. And such passionate love evaporates the moment its urgency has been received. If your anger is love's anger, it comes on strong, serves to deepen communion in love, and then dissolves instantly. It is spontaneous anger, and leaves no trace of guilt, no residue of stress.

But if you have suppressed your anger in the past, then its unexpressed energy can build up inside of you. When you let out this anger, it can be damaging. It is anger born of denial, accumulated through closure. It is not love's spontaneous anger, but simply old tension that seeks release. It is often best to let loose this kind of pent-up anger by shouting at the sky or pounding a pillow before you approach your lover.

Anger accumulated through self-suppression is a tense residue of closure, a kind of waste product, worthy of release. This kind of anger can become toxic, hurtful, and destructive. But spontaneous anger born from care and alive as love can act as a passionate thunderbolt of heart awakening, shocking and opening lovers to their heart-core.

Over days and weeks, you can practice opening as anger with your lover. Without touching, sit or stand in front of each other, and gaze into each other's eyes. Allow your breath to feel your lover's breath. You don't necessarily have to breathe in exactly the same rhythm, simply feel your lover's rhythm and quality of breath as you breathe. Don't let your eyes wander, but continue gazing and feeling deeply into your lover's eyes. Feel into your lover's heart, through any tension or closure. Do this long enough so that both of you can feel a tangible connection, heart-to-heart, of openness, trust, and love.

Then, take turns practicing anger as love. If you are to go first, begin yelling at your lover. Even if you are only pretending to be angry, yell loud and forcefully. While you shout, continue gazing into your lover's eyes, feeling into your lover's heart, and staying deeply connected in feeling-trust. In other words, stay open and feel each other feeling each other, moment by moment, even while anger's fury flows.

If your lover closes their eyes, turns away, or breathes tensely, you might want to stop shouting until he or she can come back to deep connection with you, then begin yelling again. When you can shout angrily while also feeling into your lover's heart, and your lover can stay with you, breathing fully, gazing into your eyes, and staying connected heart to heart, then switch roles. Now your lover yells at you while you both practice staying open and deeply connected in the midst of anger's energy.

Although this is only a rehearsal for the real thing, you can develop the capacity to stay open and deeply heart-connected in the midst of anger. Like standing in a storm and relishing its wild energy, you can step into the fury of your lover's anger and open fully. You can inhale the untamed, angry energy, filling your belly with the force of anger's love, while staying connected heart to heart, continuing to gaze deeply into your lover's eyes. As you both learn to feel each other, breathe each other, and open your hearts together in the midst of giving and receiving anger, your intimacy deepens as love lives larger.

Love can be alive as all emotions. Communicated from deep heart to deep heart, expressed as urgent compassion, anger has the capacity to expose a crucial moment's slumber wide open as love.

24

PERMIT YOUR
HEART'S WILD PASSION

❧

*Spanking can be an act
of closure or openness.*

For most people at most times, violent emotions are destructive. People fly into rage and say something they don't mean. They may strike out and hurt someone, regretting it later. Or, when hurt by a lover's rejection, they may mope and eat and lay in bed, rotting in the murk of self-destructive depression. Most violence is a form of self-abuse or other-abuse.

Therefore, at first, spiritual growth means cultivating compassion and less emotional violence toward yourself and others. When you begin to grow in self-awareness, you are naturally motivated toward peace and harmony. When upset or riled, you learn to take a few breaths and calm yourself down. You try to exercise kindness rather than hate, acceptance rather than judgment, joy rather than anger.

In this way, you can become harmonious—and eventually bland. Smiling and acquiescent, your depth of love-power can become forfeited for the sake of safe but shallow calmness. You may have grown from irresponsible violence to rehearsed tranquillity, but growth doesn't need to stop there.

After you have developed the capacity to breathe through your emotional reflexes and act graciously, there is another step to take. You can learn to open *as* your emotion. Rather than striking out in knee-jerk reactivity, and rather than breathing through your anger to achieve calmness, you can actually use anger, or any other emotion, as a doorway to a deeper expression of truth and love.

Remember a time when you wanted to hit someone, punch a wall, break a dish, or hurt yourself. You probably felt trapped—by your own limits or by external constraints—or you felt stuck without love. Violence is always an effort toward greater freedom or love. Openness *is* freedom and love. Even the most violent or self-destructive emotions are rooted in the heart's need for openness, to be free, to give and receive love.

When you are open, then you are able to give and receive love fully, and you are free. However, when you don't practice to open, when you are unable to live as love, then your love-energy backs up and churns as emotional mayhem. You feel trapped and alone. Your emotional energy careens and jags.

Embraced artfully, intense emotions can be a quick route to deeper openness. Anger can provide you with the sharp thunder necessary to awaken from moody distraction, if you can open your heart and really feel your love-urgency that moves as anger.

Sadness can expose your heart, too. Right now, notice any sadness you may feel. Soften your ribcage and relax your jaw so sadness can swim freely all the way through your chest. Like the ocean, softness is yielding but not weak. Yield to your sadness without collapsing. Feel the swells of sad energy in your chest, the heaves and gasps of yearning, the depth of love in your heart that opens as sadness. To open as sadness is to open as the enormous ocean of love's yearning.

Fear signals your holding. Where are you holding tense now? In your tongue, belly, between your legs? What would happen if you trusted openness and surrendered to be lived by the mystery that is life? For a moment, do your best to open completely. Relax your muscles so that life's energy can flow unimpeded through your body. Allow life to breathe you; don't add any effort to your breath. If life wants to stop breathing you, then so be it.

What are you afraid will happen if you stopped trying to think or act, right now? Find out. Trust into your deep belly, feel into your deep heart, soften your head open like a baby's smile, and find out what you think and do as you surrender open, adding no effort to life whatsoever.

Notice when you re-grasp in fear. Your thoughts or emotions or muscles move in an effort to secure your future, to achieve safety, to defend yourself against free-fall. Feel how you distrust life's immensity to live you. Feel exactly how you limit love's unbound openness in the form of your closure. Unwilling to surrender, refusing to be lived open as the entire moment, feel yourself closing in fear. Don't pull back from fear, but feel your fear as love's current shape. Occupy the feeling-shape of your fear. When you are ready to trust the mystery that is living even as your fearful shape, open.

Anger, sadness, fear—when you allow yourself to fully feel and open as all of your emotions, then your heart can find expression through all of love's textures. Some moments may feel calm and harmonious, but others may feel fitful and wild, chaotic and hot, or painfully raw. All textures open as love.

At first, you are probably destructive with your impulsive emotional reactivity, abusing yourself or others. Therefore, it is good to learn how to take a few breaths and let your emotions calm down before you act, so you can be more peaceful and harmonious. But this kind of self-soothing is only useful until you are ready and willing to open as love in the texture of all emotions.

The progression of emotional expression—from impulsive to tranquil to free—is obvious in the sexual arena. First, sex is merely get-aroused-and-spasm or needy do-you-love-me sex. Then you grow into more harmonious sex, filled with clear communication, leisurely sensuality, and nurturing support.

Finally, unwilling to cheat yourself and your lover of your deepest heart-desire, you open entirely together. You learn to give and receive love through the whole spectrum of emotions, sexing serenely, scratching like wildcats, biting like vampires, or coalescing in motionless light. You learn to love with a wide-open heart no matter how violent or calm your loving is expressed.

In certain moments, a love-motivated and heart-connected slap on the ass—even a really painful slap—can be more erotic to your lover, and more love arousing, than any words. Likewise, if your lover is about to ruin his or her life, a care-motivated smack may wake them up to love's urgency even when calm words fail. Passionately expressed love is often dangerous, but true.

However, when violent actions are *disconnected* from your heart, then you become criminally destructive. When your heart is closed and you slap somebody, you create pain and suffering, period. Laws, rules, and safe boundaries are necessary to protect everyone from unwanted violation and damage. Clear boundaries are essential if you don't trust your lover or you don't want to cause hurt or be hurt.

Once you have mastered mutual respect and safe boundaries, your trust may be ready to grow deeper. You may grow willing to hurt and be hurt as part of love's deepening. You can invite your lover to scream at you, to wail, moan, bite, and even strike you—while you both practice to feel each other deeply and stay connected heart to heart through the tryst of physical mayhem.

If you need the space to feel safe, then abide by whatever rules and boundaries create comfort for you. Say to your lover, "You are allowed to yell if you need to, but you are not allowed to touch me until you calm down." For most people, such rules are preferable to the damage afforded by heart-closed aggression.

But aggression for love's sake is passion. To ravish or be ravished by your lover sometimes requires love's violence.

If, as a couple, you and you lover have chosen to relinquish the safety of boundaries, you can practice the art of full-spectrum loving. Rather than suppressing yourself or trying to transform "bad" emotions into "good" ones, you can learn to live *all* emotions as heart-to-heart expressions of your *deepest* love, no matter how passionately your deep love moves you. This practice can only proceed fruitfully in a context of well-earned trust and real heart connection.

While lying or sitting together, gaze into your lover's eyes and practice opening together. Relax your body and breathe deeply. Feel your lover's rhythm of breath. Feel your lover's heart as your lover feels yours.

Gazing into your lover's eyes and feeling into your lover's heart, learn to notice moments of emotional closure or distancing in your lover. Perhaps your lover seems to drift away and become less present. Or, perhaps your lover's eyes cringe in fear or protectiveness. Practicing over time, you can learn to feel your lover's heart-fluctuations of openness and closure with great sensitivity.

To refine your skill, you can narrate to your lover what you feel of their heart, moment by moment: "Opening, opening, closing, opening…." After a few minutes, your lover can verbally verify your accuracy. Based on your lover's feedback, notice how well you sensed their heart's fluctuations, which can feel like the iris of a camera's shutter opening and closing, often quite subtly.

Eventually, you both grow to trust your capacities to feel each other's heart. With practice, you can accurately sense when your lover is open and totally with you, and when your lover begins to drift away or recoil behind an emotional guard. You learn to feel these shifts even when they are very slight, sudden, or rapidly changing.

When both of you have learned to feel each other's presence and openness—or lack thereof—you can begin adding more aggressive emotions to your sexual play. Whatever emotion or impulse that you don't open *as* tends to get driven underground in your psyche, where it waits to erupt unlovingly in some unexpected future moment. But if you learn to open the tender heart of your darker impulses, you will discover that their motive is actually for deeper love, trust, and openness.

Through words, touch, movement, and breath, begin to express one of your more aggressive desires during loveplay, and immediately notice the heart-fluctuations of opening and closing in both you and your lover. Continue offering your darker loving only in moments that both of you remain open and connected with each other, heart to heart. If the iris of your heart-camera shuts at all, or if your lover begins to close, then stop moving and speaking aggressively, and re-establish openness and connection by feeling and breathing together while gazing deeply into each other's eyes.

Intense pleasure can be as distracting as emotional fear. Maybe you'll discover that your lover really *likes* you to be sexually rough with him or her. As you growl and swear and playfully pin down or spank your lover, he or she may become lost in overwhelming pleasure and sexual excitement.

If your lover closes their eyes, tightens their breath, or tenses their body, reduce your aggressive expression until full feeling-contact is re-established. Look into each other's eyes. Breathe together. Relax open and feel into each other's hearts. Wait until you are both open and feeling each other's depth of love with soft bellies and trusting hearts. The point is not to arouse each other or get absorbed in excitement, but to learn to feel your lover's depth while freely incarnating all emotions.

The next step is to practice opening as unbound love, even while aggressive emotions play through your body and heart. Gaze into the pupils of your lover's eyes deeply, as if you are looking into an endless well of love. Feel the space around you in all directions, opening your skin to feel outward without bounds. Radiate love from your heart outward, not only to your lover but to everyone. Make love with the entire moment.

Feel your lover—wet skin, pointy teeth, soft lips, wild energy—and don't stop there. Feel the walls and ceiling, feel the cars on distant roads, feel all those who have died before you, and all those who will live long after you are dead. Even as you playfully tussle with your lover, as you shout or bite or scratch, open as wide as the moment goes, including everything. Every moment in total is the shape of love's opening.

If you are playing the role of *receiving* aggressive love, then breathe open larger than your lover to receive all. Open with such trust of love's force that you are taken by the thrust of the entire moment. Feel the force of existence, the intense spread of love's immensity, entering your entire body, penetrating your heart, taking you open to infinity's wideness.

If you are playing the role of *giving* aggressive love, then invade the entire moment with your feeling-consciousness like water penetrating a dried sponge open, swelling love-laden without boundaries, opening bright and full of pleasure. Enter the entire moment—and your lover—with such fullness of presence that no part can remain unspread by love's infiltration as you pervade and breathe all open.

This kind of sexual practice is a rehearsal of the same opening you can practice by yourself throughout the day and night. Over time, with or without your lover, you can learn to make love—deeply receiving, breathing, and spreading through—as the surrendered fullness of every moment wide open.

True spiritual and sexual passion requires your capacity to open as wild as the moment loves. Smacks and shouts and dark desires can wield love as powerfully as gentle kisses, placid moods, and pats on the back. Just as years may be necessary to grow from an abusive relationship into one of mutual respect and safe boundaries, long practice may be required before you are able to open freely as the entire moment, alive as the tender heart-play of love's more aggressive forces.

25

LIVE YOUR
HEART'S TRUTH

⤮

The truth is easier
to know than to feel,
and easier to feel
than to live.

Everybody knows the truth about something. For instance, most people know that it is unhealthy to eat too many sweets. Of those who know it, less feel the truth while they munch a box of cookies. Fewer still change their behavior, once and for all, on the basis of knowing and feeling the truth.

It is much harder to live the truth than to feel it or know it. Knowledge is easiest. The mind is more malleable than the emotions or the body, and so the mind is relatively swift to change. You can hear something and immediately know the truth of it. Then you can tell it to others. You can write about it. You can create a whole philosophy based on it. And still not much changes in your life. You can know the truth—for instance, exercise improves cardiovascular fitness—and then still sit on your butt.

After your mind has grasped the truth, your emotions are next to change over time. Often years of suffering are necessary before the truth of something sinks in deep enough for your tears to flow and enthusiasm to grow in response to how true something is. Yet even highly developed emotional intelligence—your capacity to feel the truth with great sensitivity and nuance—is not sufficient for real growth.

The last part of you to be transformed by truth is your body. Being more solid than your mind or emotions, your body changes last. You will *know* what you are supposed to do, and you will *feel* the truth of it, long before you are willing to *live* it with your body. You may *know* that you can't afford a new dress or another trip to Las Vegas, you may *feel* the truth making you nervous and queasy, and yet you may not be ready to *live* the truth—so you plunk down your credit card and go through the usual motions, as guilty as you may feel. Your body's habits—the motions you go through—are the most stubborn, the most rigid, and the least yielding to truth.

Because your body is the thickest part of your self-process, sex is often the last part of your life to be transformed by truth. First, you *know* that love could be the basis for sex. Then, you learn to *feel* your lover emotionally during the tumble of passion. Finally, you learn to *live* your motions as love during sex.

Even during the most erotic, pleasurable, or painful sexual moments, you can learn to breathe as love, writhe as love, thrust as love, receive as love, and speak as love. Sex can become the *doing* of love with your entire body. Sexually, and in every moment throughout the day, you can do love by opening out, feeling everybody, inhaling the entire moment full of pain and pleasure, and exhaling love to all from your heart as you go through your motions as love.

You can train your body, like a marathon runner, to go the distance as love. When you are tired and want to collapse, give love through your breath and actions just a few more minutes. Offer a smile, lend a hand, or caress your lover, for just a moment more than your habit would curtail. Over time, your life opens as love's doing, more and more.

Throughout the day, slow down and feel your heart beating. Feel deep in your heart for the source of love's flow. Let your body open as love by softening your belly and breathing in and out of your heart. Offer your deep heart to all through your breath, and allow love to move your body every moment you can remember.

How would love wash a dish? While standing at the kitchen sink, breathing love in and out of your heart, feeling outward to the moment's open edge, how does your body rub the soapy sponge across the surface of each plate?

How can you give your open heart-truth to your coworkers, even when you disagree with them? Should you smile, tell jokes, act efficient, touch them, or walk away and give them space? Day by day, practice unfolding love as your body's skill-ful offering, from your deep heart outward to the moment's open horizon.

Knowing the truth is fairly useless; feeling it is profound; living it makes all the difference.

26

RAVISH
BEYOND SAFETY

∾

Deep sexual gifting
requires, but goes beyond,
mutual respect and equality.

In the old days, men were men and women were women, or at least were supposed to be. Men were supposed to be directed, protective, and stoic. Women were supposed to be radiant, flowing, and nurturing.

Then, for good reason, women began to feel trapped by this limited feminine role. So women grew by cultivating their more masculine qualities. They wore less make-up, dressed for success, and learned to assert their direction and purpose, achieving financial and political success.

Men soon followed in expanding their breadth, realizing that they were missing out on the joys of life. Success wasn't everything. Men embraced their feminine, life-positive qualities, taking pleasure in longer hair, colorful clothing, and shameless sensuality. They learned to relax their one-pointed rigidity and play drums in the woods, flowing with music, dance, and nature.

Men and women allowed themselves to be more whole. They accepted and embraced both their inner masculine and feminine qualities. Autonomy and independence were granted and supported for each partner in a couple. A greater equality was established. Mutual respect became the foundation for a new style of relationship. All was well.

Except, eventually, successful and independent women came to complain about all the wimpy men—where were the strong men who could accept a woman's power and still have a spine of his own, not to mention enough dangerous passion to ravish her in bed? And men eventually found hardened women to be tiresome—where were the women who could be successful without guarding their heart and tensing their body, glorious women who also enjoyed the sweetness of heart-surrender?

Macho jerks and submissive housewives had grown into sensitive men who were doggedly safe and career women who were staunchly independent. But safety and independence do not touch your deepest heart-desires.

When was the last time your man was so tenderly present with you, so confident in his desire for you, that his loving blossomed your heart in bliss and took your body, unrelentingly, into deep surrender? When was the last time your woman lit up your life with her glorious love and inflamed your body with her aching, trusting, luscious pleads? When was the last time your lover, man or woman, loved you as infinity's flesh, opening you beyond Oh God, no more was there to open?

Nobody wants to go back to the old days of narrow gender roles. But for many men and women, it is time to take the next step in sexual-spiritual evolution.

The self-sufficient woman grows to invite and enjoy ravishment without safety. She practices surrendering open to be taken by her lover's depth while breathing full as the power of love-abundance. Lushly, aboundingly open, she practices to *actively* receive the massive presence of the entire moment, taking the whole of *every* moment into her body and heart as she would receive a trusted lover of passionate strength, her love blooming open wide as the living colors of all.

She already knows she can take care of herself just fine. Now, she takes care as love's all. She loves love, and she loves opening as love's bright and powerful grace. Breath by breath, she gives her body to be possessed by love, moved by love, lived by love, fiercely alive and without shame—in every moment taking all into heart, deeply, and opening as love's all, shining as love's every color, dancing as love's every texture, whether or not she is with her lover.

As successful as she chooses to be, she never forgets that achievement is an embellishment whereas love is her blood. She practices to open and be filled as full as the moment's birth, surrendering to be moved full as love's body throughout the day, dancing, sexing, and openly communing—with nature, family, and friends. All her pleasures, from her prayers to her jewelry, artfully expose her heart as bright love. Her moment-to-moment discipline is to surrender and receive all in body and heart so that love may plump her open and have its way as the glory of her life.

The sensitive man grows to risk everything for the sake of love's freedom. He realizes that freedom lies in knowing nothing, standing open as heart's depth, and giving everything. So he practices to offer his entire presence, entering each moment open with everything he's got, gently but relentlessly giving his deepest gifts—even when fear and doubt would otherwise curb him.

He offers himself so fully he is gone in the giving. Seeing through the world like reflections of a woman on a windowpane, he feels through appearances and opens out, offering all. Feeling everything, feeling *through* everything, he pervades space thick as light. He enters and opens all appearance as he would his trusting, spontaneously showing lover.

He already knows how to share. He already knows how to listen and cooperate with others. Now he learns that living free doesn't mean compromising *or* doing whatever he wants, but rather feeling all and opening as the entire showing moment, while giving his deepest gifts, whether he wants to or not—and whether or not others want him to.

Confronted by difficulties, he persists with the blood-true strength of authentic love without retracting into blunt nicety. Feeling more open than macho armor, more spacious than contrived kindness, his uncovered heart beats outward to all and pervades each moment open to the ends of time.

Modern-day spiritual culture tends to be a lukewarm miasma of stiffened women and spineless men—very efficient and quite prudent. Once you have balanced your inner masculine and feminine, after you have achieved self-sufficient wholeness, you may naturally desire to outgrow the boundaries of a merely safe and comfortable life.

Deep down, would you rather settle for safety and comfort, or open so wide you live as love's tremendum, sometimes shouting, sometimes fighting, always unprotected, your heart exposed as a free gift, your body quaking with the force of love unbound?

27

ENJOY
FLOWERY COMBAT

∽◌∾

You are attracted to
reciprocal sexual energy.

You hopefully love your friends and family as well as your lover. Your intimate relationship is unique not because of love, but due to *masculine-feminine attraction.*

Every man and woman embodies both masculine and feminine energies, although each person's proportion is unique. This proportion determines your unique sexual gifts. It also influences whom you will find sexually attractive and who will be attracted to you.

If you had to choose, would you rather have sex with someone who is radiantly alive, fresh and juicy, longing to surrender to your loving—or with someone of deep integrity who sees through to your heart and wants to take you with confidence, passion, and total presence?

If you have a more masculine sexual essence, then you will be attracted to a more feminine lover. *The feminine is light,* which feels as *love* and shines as all *life.* A feminine lover will be radiant, full of life-energy, yearning to open as love and receive your deep love. A feminine lover's smile can light up your life and inspire your heart.

A feminine lover will also say one thing while meaning another and change mind and mood like the weather. Like Mother Nature herself, the feminine force is powerful, fluid, and unpredictable; it doesn't flow along the neat lines of reason and accountability. Most women and some men have a more *feminine sexual essence.*

If your sexual essence is more feminine, then you will be attracted to a more masculine lover. The *masculine is consciousness,* which is embodied as deep and pervading *presence.* A masculine lover will be capable of taking you and ravishing you with loving intensity and depth. A masculine lover can open you wide and expose the heart of a moment with humor.

A masculine lover will also be emotionally narrow, relatively unaware of your feelings, and much more dedicated to a sense of life-mission than to intimacy with you. The masculine cares more about where it is going than who it is going with. Most men and some women have a more *masculine sexual essence.*

The sexual essence of a few men and women is exactly balanced in its proportion of masculine and feminine (although many people mistakenly believe they have a *balanced sexual essence* because they have accumulated shallow habits of sexual suppression). If your deep sexual essence is truly balanced, you will be most attracted to a lover who is your same size and strength—you will have very little desire to be taken passionately by a masculine lover, very little desire to take your feminine lover suddenly and aggressively.

If, however, you are like most people, heterosexual and homosexual, then you do *not* have a balanced sexual essence. Although everyone has some masculine and feminine characteristics—especially on the surface—deep down, in the heart of your secret sexual desires, your sexual essence is probably quite noticeably more masculine or more feminine. Deep down, you probably desire to ravish or be ravished sexually, whether or not you have the opportunity to enjoy this depth of loveplay in your life.

Because masculine and feminine attract each other like magnets, you will attract a lover who's essence is your reciprocal, a lover who, deep down, wants to take what you enjoy giving, who wants to give what you enjoy taking. But on the surface, your differences may drive you crazy.

Herein lies the delicious torture, the "flowery combat" of intimacy—the lover who really turns you on deep in your sexual heart will also really frustrate you in more superficial moments. If you have a feminine essence, then your masculine lover's deep confidence and integrity will turn you on, except when bulldozing your feelings and nit-picking the content of everything you say in a moment of conflict. If you have a masculine essence, then your feminine lover's spontaneous laughter and fluid sexual responsiveness will turn you on, except during times of whacko hysteria and unpredictable shutdowns.

In moments of deep communion, the masculine and feminine open as a singular gift—two facets of one jewel. But in more shallow moments, their surface differences can clash. When trying to communicate something verbally, for instance, the masculine wants to understand the problem and get to the point, hoping that a conversation will traverse a relatively straight path from point A to point B to point C to conclude with a solution or mutually agreed-upon resolution. The feminine enjoys talking like dancing, as a way to connect in feeling, as a way to swim together and enjoy the currents of shared energy.

In most couples, the more masculine partner gets frustrated by the feminine's loopy style of talking on and on toward nowhere in particular, while the more feminine partner is frustrated by the masculine's rigid aim and know-it-all grid of the Way Reality Is.

How can you open and love through sexual differences as doorways into deeper unity? How can moments of frustration be opened to reveal the deeper gifts?

First, take an inventory of your sexual style: Do you often compromise your *deepest* heart-desire for the sake of surface harmony and equality? Giving your lover the space to say whatever they want, in whatever way they want to say it, is a useful therapeutic exercise when practiced occasionally. It can lead to mutual understanding and feelings of being supported. But it stops short of the heart-surrendered ravishment that lies at the deep core of most intimate desire.

When equality is no longer in question, when you feel understood and supported, it is time to go deeper. There you will find the heart to the art of sexual gifting.

At your depth, you will discover a singular desire to be wide open as love, free as unbound consciousness, fearlessly alive as spontaneous gifting. Instead of compromising to satisfy your more superficial needs, you can practice to open deeply heart-one with your lover, fully alive and unbound as the moment's open display of light.

If your feminine lover is blabbing on about nothing in particular, offer your deep and unrelenting presence. Without turning away or numbing out, penetrate your feminine lover's heart with the gift of your absolute presence. Breathe, move, and gaze eye to eye as if this were your last moment alive together.

If your masculine lover has reduced life to problems, solutions, and projects, overwhelm your lover with your feminine force. Like a monsoon, like an ocean of wet light, drench your lover's body in delight; soak your lover in love's deep—and unescapable—waters.

Deep intimacy is based not on getting what you want nor on compromising equitably, but on *giving* the deepest gifts of your sexual essence. Notice your superficial masculine need to solve a problem or your superficial feminine need to connect with your partner emotionally, and instead, offer your deepest heart and open completely as the entire moment.

As the masculine partner, give your deep and undistracted consciousness as a gift, pervading your lover wide open. As the feminine partner, show your whole body alive as love's offering, inviting your lover wide open. Offer your deep sexual gifts through confession, heart-to-heart, loin-to-loin, eye-to-eye. In deep embrace and with a smile of gratitude:

He: "I am consciousness, and you are mine, my bright bitch."

She: "I am light. Take me…if you dare!"

As you and your lover merge wide open, enjoy the truth of your seeming play: Presence loves radiance, radiance loves presence. Showing as feminine light and attending as masculine consciousness, every moment relaxes open as one conscious light. As lovers, play your apparent differences with humor, opening as one, loving as two.

28

UNGUARD
YOUR SEX

〜

Layers of fear, hurt,
and anger probably surround
the gifts of your deep
sexual essence.

Are you able to give and receive love freely through your body? Does your flesh respond to sex with ripples of open delight? Does your deep heart express itself ecstatically through words of beg, moan, and command? Are you able to give yourself entirely to your lover as a gift, opening with your lover, passionately, as love without limits?

Your deepest sexual gifts may remain ungiven, unless you understand the truth of your deep desire. What do you want most in life? What do you really hope to feel, get, or give? What prospect moves your emotions the most?

If your sexual essence is more masculine, then your life is mostly motivated by a desire to be *free.*

If your sexual essence is more feminine, then your heart mostly yearns for *love.*

Everyone wants to attain more freedom *and* love—and when you are open deeper than time, freedom *is* love—but the predominant texture of your unfolding life drama is determined by the disposition of your sexual essence.

More often, with greater emotion, are you driven by the need to succeed or aching with the desire for love?

If you are not sure which you want more, freedom or love, then you may be among the few people who have a balanced sexual essence. If your sexual essence is balanced—comprised of equal amounts of masculine and feminine energies—then you equally enjoy boxing matches and love stories. You react with equal emotion to stock market fluctuations and the vacillations of your lover's attentiveness. Magazines with photos of naked bodies containing articles about political strategy and how to catch more fish rivet your attention as much as magazines with photos of the newest styles in fashion containing articles about interior decorating and how to keep passion alive in your marriage.

But if you are among the majority of people with a more masculine or a more feminine sexual essence, then you are more moved by either fights for freedom or dramas of love. Deep down, you desire a sexual partner who loves to submit to your ravishing, or one who takes you, swoons you, and ravishes you to overflowing. Someone of your same strength—with whom you break even every time you arm-wrestle—does not particularly turn you on; your most potent sexual longing is for someone who can lovingly "take" you, or someone who lovingly yields to be "taken." In fact, this play of loving surrender is the gist of some of your deepest sexual desires.

If you are like many people, then deep down you know what you want, but on the surface your daily life may seem conflicted and confused. You want to enjoy untamed sexual passion, but you spend the day stressing your body and denying your heart for the sake of a good income. Sometimes you feel driven by the masculine need to push your limits and achieve the freedom of success—often at the expense of your love life. At other times you feel bursting with the feminine fullness of love-light—or depressed by its lack, unable to really focus your life and achieve your goals.

How does this confusion happen? Why does your career or your intimate life sometimes feel artificial or bereft of great passion? What has happened to your deepest sexual gifts? What is separating you from knowing your life's true passion, your deepest purpose for being alive?

One important clue to answering these questions: Your sex may be encased. You may have acquired layers of superficial sexual energy around your deep sexual essence. You may have lost touch with your heart's deepest desires—the deepest purpose of your life—because layers of shallow energy have encased your heart. As a child, how might you have formed these shells around your heart?

Suppose you are a boy or girl born with a deep *feminine* sexual essence. The feminine is the force of life, the power of Mother Nature, the light that shines as the world. The feeling of this light is love, and every new lover shines like a radiant dawn. When you are open to your feminine energy, then you move and feel like nature. Sometimes you are alive like a sunny day, at other times like a wild monsoon. But always you are lived by love, or longing to. Because at heart you *are* love—though you might close down to it—you either shine with love's light or want to. Such is the feminine.

If you are born with a feminine sexual essence, then as a child you enjoy playing as love and light. You open as heartful flow while communing with puppies and dolls. You enjoy shining different hues of radiance while adorning your body with glittery colors, shimmering outfits, and sparkly jewelry. You want to be seen and felt as love-light because that's what your essence is.

Now, suppose you are a few years old and your little sister is born. Your parents find her prettier than you. She's the *cute* one and now you're the *achiever*. For Christmas, your little sister gets the sequined ballet tutu and you get the microscope. Although you like microscopes, you still feel crushed. She gets the bangles and ribbons and you get the encyclopedia. You like to read, but your heart still feels trampled. Even though you are smart, you want your love-light acknowledged and cherished.

Privately, your parents try to reassure you: "Your sister is pretty, but you're on your way to something great. Prettiness is only skin deep, but you're going to *go* somewhere in your life."

"Yes," you repeat to yourself as you enviously watch your sister bouncing around and bringing joy to the home in her bangles and tutu, "I'm *going* somewhere." Your feminine heart, your shining light of love, is aching to be seen. So to buffer yourself from the pain of being invisible, you begin to identify with your masculine, your sense of direction.

The masculine seeks to be aligned with a deep sense of purpose or mission, to break free and open into success, rather than to open and flow as the radiance of deep love. Everyone enjoys both free consciousness *and* bright love, but your true sexual fulfillment depends on clarifying the deepest desires of your unique sexual essence.

Because your little sister is getting all the attention for being the radiant one, your heart feels crushed. Your light is unseen. You hurt inside. So to buffer your hurt you begin to identify with your masculine sense of direction: "I'm going to be a scientist." It's one thing to choose a career because you love science; it's quite another to choose a direction in life as a reaction to hurt, as a shell to protect your crushed heart.

For the next several years, you build a shell of thin masculine directionality around your deep and wounded feminine essence. You become directed with a vengeance. In spite, you tell your sister, "You are pretty … pretty stupid!" Secretly, you are dying for others to recognize the beauty of your heart's radiance, but outwardly you despise "shallow women" who lack direction.

In high school, you are the girl "most likely to succeed." Everything about you—the way you walk, talk, and dress—is colored by the shell of masculine I'm-going-somewhere energy surrounding your crushed heart of deep love and radiance. Eventually, you notice that the boys aren't as attracted to you as to the radiant energy-girls, the cheerleaders and pompom girls, the bouncy, sparkly girls. You want boys to want you, so your next shell begins to form.

You begin to imitate the feminine radiance of the attractive girls. You wear the glossy lipstick they are wearing. You buy the same brand of shapely jeans. You check your butt in the mirror before going to school and learn to walk and pose like the popular girls. This isn't the natural expression of your deep feminine light, but a needy imitation of a superficial aspect of feminine display.

Now, you have a body-shape-obsessed feminine shell surrounding a purpose-obsessed masculine shell surrounding your crushed heart of truly and deeply radiant love-light. What kind of high-school boy will you attract? Since sexual energies always attract their reciprocal, you will attract a boy with a thin masculine shell around a thin feminine shell around a wounded but truly purposed deep masculine essence.

Imagine you were such a boy. As a child, your deep *masculine* sexual essence is identified with direction, purpose, and seeking freedom amidst challenges. Your parents tell you to be careful not to fall off the porch—so you meet the challenge by walking right on the edge. Your friends can jump off a six-foot-high roof—so you try to jump off one ten feet high. Because you are identified with the masculine, you want to be acknowledged for your sense of purpose and your capacity to break through limits into freedom.

But suppose your father is an alcoholic and prone to abusive behavior. You assert your direction, and he beats you. You want to leave dinner early to play with a friend and your father smashes you, yelling, "This is my house and you'll do what I say, or else!" Anytime you present your perspective, your vision, or your direction, you are beaten or yelled at.

Eventually, to avoid the pain of being hurt, you learn to squelch your sense of direction. You learn to become ultra-sensitive to your father's mood. You learn to flow around him in order to avoid getting smashed. In other words, you develop a feminine shell around your deep masculine essence.

Out of fear, you learn to flow. This isn't your healthy feminine openness to love. This isn't your natural feminine sensitivity to life force and energy. This is a shell of protection surrounding your deep sexual essence. You have silenced the true assertion of your deep masculine sense of purpose and have built a guarded shell of feminine caring and flow.

"Sure, dad. I love you, dad." But the strength of your deep sexual essence withers. Your denied masculine heart becomes weak and hollow. You have learned to adapt to your father's sense of direction, but have lost touch with yours.

In high school, you realize that the caring flow-boys don't attract girls like the tough and self-directed go-boys. The girls seem to be attracted to the motorcycle bad guys, the football quarterbacks, and the confident class president. So you buy the same cigarettes the tough guys smoke and practice puffing them with tough-guy mannerisms. You learn to walk and talk like you know where you are going. You learn to fake confidence even though deep down you are terrified and lost.

So, naturally, the boy with a deep-but-wounded masculine essence covered by a feminine flow-shell covered by a masculine go-shell is attracted to the girl with the deep-but-crushed feminine essence covered by a masculine go-shell covered by a feminine flow-shell.

Reciprocals always attract, layer by layer. On the outside, he puffs his chest and she wiggles her butt. Underneath that, he carefully avoids confrontation and gives way to her direction, while she reminds herself that knowing who she is and where she is going is more important than being attractive. At heart, his sense of deep purpose remains stultified and her sense of deep love-light aches with the desire to be recognized and cherished.

If they get married, their shells form a tangled union. Their encased sexual essences remain untouched while their shells feel alternately needed and rejected. She wants him to make more money and decisions, or she gives up and hopes to make them for herself. He wants her to revel more in sexual beatitude, or he gives up and hopes to find what he wants in a mistress. She can feel his fear of confrontation and loses trust in him. He can feel her lack of trust, her body's tension and her heart's protection, so he loses desire for her. Eventually, they get divorced.

Now, rejected and alone, she builds yet *another* shell of protection: "I'm going to put relationships on the back burner while I build my own career. I'll never depend on a man again!" While it may be healthy for everyone to develop his or her own career, to do so based on fear and heart-protection is a clear sign of a masculine shell at work.

He, too, adds another shell to his encased essence: "I've just thrown away decades of my life trying to support a wife and family, always postponing what I really want to do. It's time to enjoy my life. I'm going to travel—maybe to somewhere beautiful like Bali or Hawaii—and just go with the flow. I'm going to live spontaneously. If I meet a woman I like, I'll stay with her as long as it feels good, and then I'll move on to whatever comes next."

If his spontaneity were to flow from his deep heart-purpose, then it would be healthy and fresh, an expression of love alive. But in this case, his need to flow and keep moving is a strategy for avoiding depth, direction, and commitment—it's a shell.

He becomes a sensitive, flowing, fun-loving man, indecisive and utterly lost to his life's deep purpose, as she becomes a very successful and clearly directed woman whose heart yearns behind closed doors. Of course, since their shells are reciprocal, flowy men and directed women like this are attracted and get together, only to be disappointed all over again.

Your deep sexual essence may be more masculine, more feminine, or balanced. Begin to open to its depth by first admitting to yourself your *deepest* desires. In your deep heart, are you more moved by the search for freedom or the search for love? Are you more moved when your lover trusts your direction or praises your radiance? Or does it all feel about the same?

Imagine that you are in bed with your lover, who is quite successful and self-sufficient in their life. Your lover looks into your eyes with deep longing and says, "I'll do anything you want me to. I want to open and give myself to you to take as you desire. I'll follow you anywhere." Does it turn you on for your lover to trust your deep integrity so much that he or she is willing to utterly surrender to you? If so, then you have a more masculine sexual essence. You are turned on by your lover's trust of your deep integrity and direction.

Imagine, instead, that your lover looks into your eyes with deep desire, praising you from their heart, "You are so beautiful. I love you so much. I want you. I want to possess every part of you." Does this turn you on? Does it turn you on for your lover to see your true beauty and want to possess you, desiring to dive into the glory of your open radiance and enter the deepest chambers of your heart? If so, then you have a more feminine sexual essence. You are turned on by your lover's heart-spoken praise and passionate desire for your deepest love-light.

Of course, your superficial shells of protection may speak louder, for now, than your deepest desires. You may feel confused or divided inside. Your accumulated guards and various sexual defenses may resist the very actions that would allow your deep essence to fully open so you could grow to give your deepest gifts to your lover and the world.

No matter how many shells of protection you have, whether you are a man or a woman, if deep down you have a *masculine* sexual essence, then you will feel free only when you *discover your heart's deepest purpose and align your life's mission and relationships with your deepest integrity.* Then, with time's revelation, you can live to realize there is nowhere to go but open.

If you have a *feminine* sexual essence, you will only feel the love you know is possible when *you surrender your body open to give and receive love, offering the unprotected radiance of your heart.* Then, as love's power blooms through your life, your yearning opens fully as love alive as all.

What do you most deeply desire to give? What have you always desired to give, despite your imitation roles? Confess your protection, risk letting go of your carefully built shells, and offer the life-mission or love-light you have always wanted to give, from your heart. Give your integrity, your love, your gifts, *entirely.* Open so wide your clarity of purpose is unstoppable, your radiance of love abounds. Live free, love fully, and die unshelled.

29

DON'T SETTLE
FOR FULFILLMENT

෨෨

When some moment seems
particularly miraculous,
open through it to your
deepest truth.

Some people have felt the incomparable ecstasy of achieving their wild-
est dreams, winning millions of dollars in a lottery or garnering a Nobel
Prize. Many mothers have held newborn infants to their breasts, overwhelmed
in the bliss of unimaginable love. These kinds of moments are what make life
utterly deluding.

The divine masculine in you is infinite consciousness. When you lose touch
with it, you seek infinity in the confines of your life: your bank account, your
fame, your achievements. Anything that gives you a whiff of breaking free into
unbound no-stress—a touchdown, an ejaculation, or great professional victory—seems to be a source of almost sacred bliss.

The divine feminine in you is the force of life, the abundant energy, or
light, of love. When you lose touch with it, you seek blissful fullness through
the portals of your body, your senses, your relationships. Anything that over-
whelms you in love's fullness—from your children, to sex, to your favorite
chocolate—can seem almost divine.

Every moment is an opportunity to open as your true divine nature, which is infinite consciousness and bountiful love. Most people, however, lose touch with their deepest openness. Feeling a lack, they become devotees of the scratch that fulfills their itch. They worship substitutes. The masculine literally worships achievement, understanding, and success, while the feminine is often devoted to angelic children, heavenly fabrics, succulent flavors, and love-promising relationships.

The addictive quality of minor substitutes such as sports and shopping can be strong; the deluding power of grand substitutes can be extraordinary. A devout parent can spend decades cherishing his or her children before time takes them away. A devoted businessperson can spend the better part of a lifetime thriving on the juice of freedom's challenge before motivation wanes and life's flatness stares him or her in the face.

Grand substitutes are whatever life-functions you mistake for life's truth: eating, sexing, raising children, earning money, acquiring possessions, expressing creative impulses, cultivating relationships. The truth is, if you think that one or another of these functions is particularly divine, you are in for great suffering. You can *express* divine love and freedom through any of these activities or relationships. But if you think they are your *source* of bliss, then you become like a drug addict, dependent on a substitute that will inevitably cease to satisfy.

If you have a more feminine sexual essence, you are built so certain things are shaped to press your love-button. Don't mistake the thing for the love. When you hold your infant against you in seemingly perfect love, open *as* this love. *Be* the immensity of love your beautiful child evokes. Remember that there are plenty of lonely women with empty hearts who were once full-blush mothers, overflowing with bliss amidst their children's laughter.

If you have a more masculine sexual essence, it is easy to spend hours, days, even years totally engrossed in the tasks at hand. Like a monk in prayer, your life can become devoted to the image of your salvation: the discovery, realization, creation, or achievement that will set you free. But if you ever have attained your goals, you know that the bliss of achievement passes—however noble your cause—and once again you look for a way to be more deeply liberated from stressful motivation.

Full as immense love, you can share love's bliss with your children without strangling them in your neediness. Open as free consciousness, you can offer your gifts to the world through your mission without stressing to succeed.

Every act and relationship in your life is an offering. Give yourself fully. Open as limitless love and boundless freedom. Always give from the unbound fullness of your open heart. Do not reduce your family or career into grand substitutes for the bliss that is your very being.

In moments that seem miraculous, don't settle for the glow of interim fulfillment. Your child's embrace or your career's fruition can, for a while, seem overwhelmingly sufficient. Even so, practice being abundantly full and utterly released in *every* moment, because this is who you are. You are born to live as unbound love and openness. You are born to live as the offering of your deepest gifts. Don't burden your children and vocation with the obligation to delude you for a lifetime.

30

BE FREE AS
LOVE NOW

❧

*Doing anything only leads
to more doing and never
fulfills your deepest desires.*

The need to *do* defines your life. Something is missing, your life isn't quite complete, and so you *do*.

Regardless of what you do, your life will be briefly intense and quickly forgotten, seemingly important and not quite satisfying—a fleeting memory of pleasure and pain, gain and loss, health and disease, love and loneliness. Then you will die, as all those before you have. Genghis Khan, Princess Diana, and Frank Sinatra are dead. Evaporated from this world. Eventually the sun will explode and the earth will vaporize. Everything that has come together comes apart. Guaranteed.

And yet putting things together—your business, your intimate relationship—seems so important. The masculine in you is riveted to the adventure of success and failure. Do, do, do, do, do, and always the question is, "Am I succeeding or failing?" Always waiting for that day in the future when success will be enough and you can finally live the way you want to.

By that time, you will have trained your attention to adhere to *doing*, as if life goes somewhere. But nothing makes a real difference in old age—or at any age—but depth. You can be a millionaire at twenty or eighty, and still your life will feel empty and meaningless unless you have learned to feel beneath the surface of your doings, into the open being that some call God, Truth, or Love.

Doing or not, life is deep. Doing or not, this moment is open, infinitely full, without bounds. You are already free, but the masculine in you thinks you need to earn it, and so you *do.*

The feminine in you is enmeshed in the drama of love and unlove. Day by day, year by year, the feminine feels, "I'm loved, not loved, loved, not loved, loved, not loved ..." as if the entire world revolved around your emotional fulfillment. As if you could wait out the bad times, and then great intimacy will become possible. As if your lover will grow, or you will find the right partner who could really love you like you want.

Meanwhile, the pain of emptiness echoes in your body, so you *do* to fill it. Eat. Talk. Shop. Yearn. "I will never be loved." "I am loved." "Am I loved?" Day by day, your hope for love wears down, until finally you settle for a relationship that is good enough, but not as good as you know love can be. And so you wait, unopen and unfulfilled. "My partner isn't giving me the love I want, so I'll hold back my love, too."

Waiting for love or doing anything to be loved is as fruitless as a fish swimming in the hope of getting wet. Already, love is who you are. Love is that which is living your life, breathing your breath, moving your body and all bodies.

Love is wanting to open your heart right now. You can feel love's desire to flow through your entire body, this very moment. You have to refuse love to lack it. You have to close your heart, suppress your breath, and tense your body to feel lonely and empty. As long as you are doubting or self-guarded, no *doing* leads to more love.

Yet, as you look around you, almost everyone is doing something, stressfully. Trying to earn a sense of freedom. Yearning for deeper love.

It seems that life is about *doing.* It is true that life is action, always changing. But no doing can get you the real freedom and trustable love that you most deeply want, *ever*. Doing can possibly get you more money. Doing can help you meet people and improve your skills in relationship. But even so, amidst money and relationships, you will still feel unfulfilled unless you stop closing in fear and relax open, as you are, right now.

Like a fish in an infinite ocean of clear liquid, feel into the space around you as if it were water. Inhale and exhale as if you were breathing water's thickness, drawing in and releasing the buoyant clarity surrounding you. Feel the water pervading your body, softening your feeling-skin open.

From your heart, feel outward through the water of space. Feel sound as a vibration in this water, like loud music might vibrate your gelatinous core. Feel the objects around you through the water of space. Open so your feeling extends through the water on and on. As you feel out into the water around you, does your feeling end?

Is there a boundary to this moment? As you feel beyond your immediate vicinity, does your feeling hit a wall, or does feeling open out beyond visibility, like an ocean's open clarity? Feel through and beyond your vicinity as water without bounds, endlessly opening.

While opening, remaining utterly sensitive, soft, soaked through by the water. Your heart opens like love-jelly vibrating with every sound, lit up by every color and ray of light. As people come near you, feel the water between you and them as it thickens or swirls, touching your heart differently with each person's whirl of texture and emotion. From your heart, feel all.

Extending your feeling without bound, open. Full of all experience, open. As the entire moment, open.

Open, you are free, and your work can enlarge freedom for others. Open, you are love, and your relationships can extend love through the world. But if you are waiting for a future day to open as you are, then nothing you *do* will bring the freedom and love for which you most deeply yearn.

Many people you know have earned plenty of money and had numerous relationships, yet their hearts are neither free of fear nor full of love. *Doing* is a fact of life. But its rewards are overrated. Open your heart now, and be free, as this entire moment, alive as love.

31

SHINE AS
LOVE'S LIGHT

❧

*Light is what
love looks like.*

When a person falls in love, she becomes radiant. She shines with love. Her eyes sparkle. Her skin glows. This is because love is what light feels like.

Love is the feeling of light. Light is the appearance of love.

The feminine in everyone is identified with love-light.

If you have a more feminine sexual essence, or if you are, in the moment, identified with your feminine, then you want to be seen as light and felt as love. Does gold or silver jewelry bring out the shine in your eyes today? Does a red or blue blouse most magnify your natural radiance?

The feminine is excruciatingly sensitive to the way adornments can serve to amplify or diminish your whole body's openness to energy and your heart's display of light. Wearing one pair of shoes or another pair—which may seem almost identical to a more masculine person—can mean the difference between a tawdry and a brilliant day for the feminine.

However, nothing releases the natural light of your feminine heart more than love. A person with a feminine essence can be a successful CEO, a great scientist, or the leader of a country, yet seem drab and unhappy unless love is flowing through her open heart.

The masculine heart responds most fully when aligned with a mission to advance freedom, including financial, artistic, or spiritual freedom. The masculine heart often opens deepest when facing death, or when yielding open beyond what can be known, beyond all things, opening as the freedom beyond all form.

The feminine *is* form, the light-appearance of all things, all life-power, alive as love and showing as every shape and texture and relationship. Thus, the feminine heart is moved most by all that is alive, by the coming and going of bodies, by life's dramatic ebb and tide, by the living flow of love in relationship.

Success, direction, mission, achievement, insight, clarity—these things are important to all people. But, right now, which prospect *opens your heart* more: Donning gorgeous dress and wild jewelry and dancing with your lover and closest friends to your favorite music, or sitting in a room alone without moving for many hours, practicing "ego death" and contemplating emptiness?

Danced by music's fullness, heart and body surrendered as love alive, the feminine is availed the same "oh" of openness that the masculine is afforded during moments of insight into no-self. Communing with the blissful taste of fine chocolate can be as overwhelming to the feminine as a football team's sudden death playoff can be for the masculine.

Feminine spiritual growth is about opening to receive all—all people, all situations, the massive presence of the entire moment—deep into your heart, surrendering open to breathe and move as the full force of love, aboundingly alive, appearing as all. Whereas the masculine grows by realizing identity with emptiness, boundless consciousness, the unchanging ever-present witness of life, the feminine grows by realizing identity with ever-changing light, radiant love, or the very love-fullness of all life and every moment.

The masculine craves unchanging nothingness—if not as eternal consciousness, than at least in post-ejaculative peace or zoned out in front of the TV. The feminine *is* drama, volatile passion, an ocean of tumultuous and ever-fluid light, changing shades, dark and dazzling, concealed and exposed, longing to be seen, felt, entered so deeply as to be overflowed beyond fullness.

Emptiness and quietude are masculine obsessions. The masculine often wants to resolve feminine turmoil and conclude in unadorned openness, the one taste that feels like home to the masculine. But the feminine opens as cinnamon and garlic, as salty, sweet, and bitter, as every possible flavor.

The feminine has no motive to resolve emotions as if ending life's drama were a goal. Feminine love-light *is* life. Friendships, love stories, dining, shopping, the intimate theater of hurt and joy, of love lost and gained—the feminine is at home in the fullness of emotion and sensuality, not the empty, unborn void from which the masculine witnesses life. Rapturous devotion, ecstatic dance, wrought-up song, sexual revelry in light's bliss and love's tides—these are among the idioms of feminine openness.

Brief pleasure, however, is not the same as deep openness. For instance, the masculine can drink a beer, watch TV, or have an orgasm, and the vacuous pleasure is fairly short-lived. Likewise, the feminine can talk on the phone with a dear friend, go shopping, or dance outrageously in the kitchen, and the feeling of vivacious fulfillment won't last for too long. Brief pleasures might provide a doorway, but then you can *practice* to sustain and deepen openness.

If you love to dance, for instance, you can use dance as a spiritual practice. Perhaps you can remember a time when you were dancing and felt wide open, as if you were surrendered to the force of love and life as it was dancing you. How did you move? What did you feel in your heart?

As love dancing alive, how do your feet make contact with the ground? What do you feel in your legs? What do you feel *between* your legs and in your loins, sexually, energetically, as you dance open as the force of life? How do you feel in your belly and chest as the music enters you and moves through you? What expressions show by way of your face and arms and hands? How does love move through and radiate as your entire body?

Enjoy dancing as a true spiritual practice by discovering this: How to dance now so that your heart beams open and your entire body breathes alive as love's fullness? How can you dance now so your body and heart open to receive every moment deeply and your life shows as love *all day*? How could you dance through the years so that even as your body ages and withers, your heart opens ever more full, as wide as the moment, shining as love's radiance to all?

Feminine spiritual practice—sacred dance, for example—requires the same discipline as does solitary meditation. Although openness is who you are, closure is what you tend to do. Sacred dance, like meditation, is the undoing of your habits of fear and closure so your life blossoms open as a blessing of love.

As you dance, notice how the shape of your hands and the position of your fingers affect the openness of your heart. Where in your mouth does your tongue rest, and what shape are your lips—smiling, frowning, relaxed, pressed tight—so that love's energy flows most freely from your heart throughout your whole body to open as the entire moment shining as all?

Opening to receive the full moment and radiate your heart's full light, how do your feet make contact with the ground when your heart loves the earth through your legs? How do your feet touch the ground with angry love? Sweet love? Yearning love?

How do you dance when you remember someone you love, moving your hips with the sorrow and joy that has moved your heart? How does the back of your neck open when you remember your ancestors? How do your knees and throat open when you remember all those who need your love? How do you dance as a devotional offering, opening to receive the pain of all others, dancing their suffering, offering your deepest heart-blessing as you open? If you were dancing as a divine goddess, how would you dance?

Although sacred dance can open your body to great bliss, you will also discover how you close to love's fullness. You will come upon ways you hate to move and postures you hate to hold.

Feel through these movements and postures that you hate. Perform them over and over as you practice to open so that love can flow through your entire body and outward to all. Allow love's energy to tickle your closures, warm your stiffness, and gush you open. Together with your feminine-essence friends, you can oblige each other to open as love, to gently press love through your fear and protection, to feel each other and love each other—especially while you are doing movements and postures you hate.

Just as you can dance your own body open as love, you can practice dancing your friends' bodies open. You can feel their closure into your body, so they have the opportunity to feel you dancing their unfoldment.

Stand in front of a friend and actively open to receive her into you. Breathe her shape, her guardedness, her darkness, deeply into your heart. Take her qualities into the form of your body. Breathing as her, move as her. Feeling her love and her fear, dance her open.

Allow your friend to feel you opening as her. Writhe your pelvis to open as love through her shape. Feeling as if her body was yours, practice opening every cell, from your toes to your fingers to the top of your head, and *every* part in between, especially the parts that feel dark or closed. Receive your friend's shape as yours and dance open as her, exposing your hearts, unlocking love for the sake of all.

As you dance, with practice, you can feel yourself alive not only as one friend, but as all. Breathe in all pain, all closure, all tension. Feel your body as love's body, your heart pumping the blood of all, your breath receiving and giving for the sake of all. Feeling all, breathing all, open as all. Dance alive as every dark and bright shade of light, moving open as every fearful and lonely body. Open as every texture of love, rageful love, worshipful love, bitter love, yearning love. Open as all, as every, as love.

Sometimes you will feel divine life coursing through your open body. Other times you may feel clogged with black sludge, making you want to curl up in the corner and puke. Either way, practice to open as much as you can. Breathe deeply, and do your best to stay open with your friends in loving, eye-to-eye, heart-to-heart feeling-contact. Or, if you are alone, breathe and feel open, staying in touch with the love that wants to flow through you. No matter how closed you may feel, you can practice breathing and surrendering open, offering yourself to be moved by love as an offering in every moment.

Practice opening while you dance and also randomly throughout the day. Moment by moment, with or without music, breathe all pain and pleasure through your heart in and out, allowing love to open through your closures—through everyone's closures—offering your body open, full as the moment.

Practice this fullness especially when you would rather not, when your body is closed down, when you would rather withhold your love from everyone, from someone, or from yourself. Don't just give yourself permission to be full; *oblige* your surrender as love's fullness, through your entire body, breathing and moving and living open as love's all.

You can practice this way anytime, not only when you are hurt, but also when you are full of pleasure. As chocolate melts on your tongue, or while your lover kisses your lips, allow love's pleasure to fill your body. Notice if your pleasure-energy stops anywhere—if your belly is tense or your womb feels numb or your toes aren't wiggling—and breathe your body full open. Stay open and feeling-connected with those who may be around you, looking into the eyes of your friends or lover as you practice breathing and magnifying and overflowing as love's pleasure.

Allow chocolate pleasure to soften your tongue and open your throat and fill your belly, while receiving into your melting heart the sweetness of the living moment. Breathe pleasure-energy through every inch of your body, allowing love to radiate abundantly from your full heart to all. Give chocolate love through your entire body—through your smile, your bright eyes, your happy thighs, and yummy sounds—to your friends and outward to all.

As your lover kisses you, receive love's pleasure deeply, breathing your heart open, receiving the kiss pressed into you by the very lips of the full moment's presence. Kissed to love's depth, offer your undulations and moans as heart-gifts to your lover and to all. Breathe as your body, breathe as your lover's body, and breathe as all bodies, feeling all and opening alive as every form, full as love's pleasure.

Since every person embodies both masculine and feminine, every man and woman can benefit from opening themselves as both emptiness and fullness. Sitting in the open silence of meditation and surrendering open as love's dance are useful for everyone. Nevertheless, observation, insight, meditation, and solitude always have and always will characterize the masculine approach to openness. And, to some degree, these practices always have and always will be a source of great boredom for the feminine.

The feminine moves and breathes as life. Shines as every shade. Opens as every flavor. The feminine is unbounded *as* life. Alive as love, dancing as all bodies, the feminine opens as all.

32

PLAY SEXUALITY
AS ART

෨෨

The masculine directs,
the feminine invites.

H ow do you keep passion alive in an intimacy, even with all the daily
decisions and chores that need to be done? To understand the art of
sexual gifting, you can begin by feeling the nuances of how talking and acting
affect your lover. As you grow more open, your every word and gesture can be
a gift to all—or not.

Openness includes all possible qualities, including masculine and feminine. The feminine is life force, the effusion of light and love that dances as
your body, emotions, and the shine of the entire moment. The masculine is
consciousness itself, the no-thing of simple presence, the emptiness or silent
witness of this moment's show.

As you deepen your capacity to open as consciousness, you come to know
who you are and how to live your deepest purpose in a world of change. The
capacity to know your deepest purpose and consciously navigate your life, as
well as the lives of others, is part of your masculine capacity, whether you are
a man or a woman.

In today's modern culture, most people still glorify masculine purposeful-ness and vilify the force of attraction that is inherent in the feminine display of life. Every morning as you wake from deep sleep, you can feel how this moment's light attracts and invites consciousness into life's show. In every moment, the feminine display invites the masculine into action. In today's anti-feminine culture, however, men and women are supposed to stand back and direct rather than offer life's full showing, the *feeling* of life, as an invita-tion for action.

For instance, you are supposed to direct someone, even your lover, by telling him or her what to do rather than by inviting their action through expressing life's feeling. Your masculine statement, "Please turn on the heat," is considered more honest than your feminine invitation-through-feeling-expression, "I'm feeling really cold." People who are particularly proud of their masculine capacity consider this feminine style of invitation to be manipula-tive and covert.

In the realm of business and friendship, using your masculine to direct someone toward specific action is often the most effective way to get some-thing done. But in the realm of intimacy, where the flow of sexual energy often defines the texture of the moment, your speech is more a matter of erotic art than functional efficacy.

How can your style of talking increase or diminish sexual flow? Sexual passion flows between two energetic poles: masculine and feminine. Similar to the electrical flow between positive and negative poles, or the magnetic flow between north and south poles, sexual energy always flows between the two poles of masculine and feminine. If you and your partner are both in your masculine—you are both offering the gift of direction, for instance—then sexual flow stops because there is no feminine gift of invitation to complete the polarity. This is equally true in homosexual and heterosexual relationships.

When you give direction, you stand as a masculine pole. For instance, sup-pose you are the feminine partner in an intimate relationship. When you tell your masculine lover what to do by specifying a course of action—"Would you please take off your shoes?"—your masculine energy won't allow a flow of polarity with your lover's masculine. You have sexually neutralized the flow. Your masculine lover will feel turned off. To re-create an arc of sexual polarity, either you or your lover can offer the feminine energy of invitation. You can freely choose who plays the masculine pole and who plays the feminine in every moment. Whose masculine presence—and whose feminine radiance—is more desired in the flow of sexual passion?

The effect of sexual neutralization through lack of polarity and can be quite subtle, although it accumulates over time. Again, suppose you are the feminine partner in a relationship. If you repeat masculine directiveness often enough—"Can you take out the garbage? Would you pick up the kids from school?"—you can inadvertently create a complete lack of sexual attraction, even repulsion, between you and your lover. Your masculine lover needs to feel your *feminine* energy in order for an arc of sexual attraction to flow and pull him toward you.

If you want to offer yourself as the gift of feminine energy in your intimacy, then offer the energy of pull rather than push. Invite action through expressing your full feeling-experience rather than direct it by sculpting a course through your action-specifying question. Open a door, but don't ask your lover to come through it. Allow the open door to be an invitation—if you want to maintain the full flow of sexual polarity.

Rather than, "Would you please take off your shoes?" open the door with, "I'd love to touch your feet." Rather than, "Can you take out the garbage?" invite action by revealing your sensual world with, "I'm beginning to smell the garbage." Rather than, "Would you pick up the kids from school?" flesh out your living experience by expressing, "I'm worried about the kids waiting at school." Simply invite action by expressing your feeling-experience, and allow your masculine lover to specify what course of action to take or not.

Whoever specifies the course of action by directing it—through words or behavior—carries the masculine energy in the moment. If you say, "Could you fill the car with gas?" then you are specifying your partner's action through your request. But if you say, "I'm worried that the car is running out of gas," then you are creating an invitation for action by expressing your feeling. You open a space in the moment for your lover to fill with masculine direction. You offer the water of possibility for your lover to enter and navigate.

This difference between directing and inviting your partner may seem small, but over time it can make a big difference in the flow of sexual desire. You may get the action you want faster through directing your lover, but you may also depolarize and weaken the arc of passion.

Your masculine lover, unfamiliar with offering his navigation as a gift, may actually prefer that you navigate for yourself and specify what you want in terms of clear direction—and then lose sexual interest in you without knowing why. You can decide which is more important moment by moment, functional effectiveness or sexual polarity. Then you can artfully choose the efficiency of specifying direction or the attraction of maintaining polarity. You can choose to direct or invite.

You can *love* your partner when both of you are expressing your masculine and trying to direct the moment. But how you play your sexuality together all day—energized in attractive polarity or neutralized in efficiency—imbues your bodies in bed at night. You will only want to *ravish* or *be ravished* by your lover when one of you is lovingly open as radiant, surrendered, untamed, feminine life force and the other is lovingly open as masculine consciousness, the force of clear purpose, confident navigation, and utter presence.

If you relinquish your directiveness to offer your feminine gift of invitation, then in order to create two sexual poles your lover must reciprocate by animating the masculine gift of conscious navigation. Your lover must be present and clear, noticing what needs to be done, and then following through with integrity. You wouldn't want to relinquish your masculine navigation if your lover was scattered, unaware, or weak.

If you are the masculine partner, you can deepen your presence by knowing your deep purpose. Ask yourself, "Why am I alive? What must I do or become so that when I die I can die complete, with a smile on my face, knowing I've given everything I have to give?" What must you do today, so that when you go to sleep tonight you know you have given everything, loved as deep as you can, offered the most genuine gifts you have to give? To live this way day by day is the way to prepare for death. When you can align your daily actions with the calling of your deepest purpose, then you can live with honor and without regret.

Free of feeling burdened, you can act with clarity and precision. If your deep purpose involves getting married and raising a family, then you can pick up the children and take out the garbage impeccably and without resentment because they are part of your deep calling, a part of the way you give your deepest gifts, day by day.

Otherwise, if you aren't in touch with your deep calling and the way you must offer your love while alive, you will feel undirected by depth. Your course will be ambiguous. Your decisions will lack commitment. You will oblige your feminine lover to animate the masculine energy in the relationship because your clarity and direction are lacking. With your sense of direction collapsed into your lack of purpose, you will do things you don't really want to.

Without a deep sense of purpose to direct your daily life, you will be directed by externals—financial need, your children's needs, your lover's needs—and you will begin to blame them for your lack of fulfillment. You will feel trapped in obligations, and your resentment will show. You will hold back in your relationships with your lover and family, not really wanting to be there, unsure what else to do, mired in ambiguity, guilt, and anger. Your actions will lack integrity and follow-through. Your feminine lover won't be able to trust you in everyday life or open to you sexually.

When you practice to open deeply, and thus allow your deep purpose to emerge through your life, then your actions spring from a profound confidence. You do what you deeply feel you must do, from your heart. You give your depth and your love fully, without resentment or withdrawal, in your chosen relationships. You are lovingly—and intensely—present.

Your consciousness is clear and unambiguous. Your actions are precise and taken to completion. A deep sense of mission guides your life, and therefore you are with your lover only when you deeply desire to be. Your lover can feel your intensity of purpose, your undistracted desire, your unambiguous presence. As in any moment of masculine clarity, when you are with your lover, you are fully *there*.

Where is your attention now? If your attention is mostly drawn to the itch on your cheek, then your lover will feel your consciousness as deep as your scratch. If your attention is feeling deeply into your lover's heart, breathing as if her suffering were yours, then your eyes, gestures, and breath will convey deeper presence to her. She will trust your deep and loving gaze more than your distracted cheek scratching.

You can strengthen your masculine presence—and thus attract your lover's trust and radiant surrender—by deepening your attention. Take a moment now and notice your thoughts. Try to feel where your thoughts are coming from. Relax for a moment and feel a single thought coming and going. Feel where it comes from and where it goes to, and then feel open as this space. Feel deeper as this space, opening where your thoughts come from and dissolve.

You can practice the same way with your emotions. Feel the "place" where you feel your emotions. Whatever emotions you may be feeling, feel *where* you are feeling, and open as this place. Feel open as where you feel, no matter what emotions you feel there.

Notice how everything in this moment, including your body, is *appearing*. Remember how it feels to have your body appearing in a dream, as if it were really your body. Then the dream fades, that particular body appearance dissolves, and another body that seems to be yours begins appearing in your next dream, or when you awaken. With practice, you can feel your body *appearing* right now. Like a thought or an emotion or a body in a dream, your body is appearing to your notice now—you may even lose notice of it while you concentrate in a task.

With practice, feel open as the place where your body appears now, the same place where your dreams appear, the place where this whole moment appears. Relax open as this place of appearance. Relax open so deeply that your body, thoughts, and emotions seem to be magically arising, appearing, shining as a luminous display that you can feel and see.

Feel your deepest sense of purpose. If you don't yet know your deepest purpose, feel where you imagine you would feel it if you could. Feel open as this deep place where you would feel your most profound sense of purpose, your heart's deepest desire.

Offer the same feeling-depth to your lover. Practice feeling into your lover, looking into her eyes and feeling into her deeply, so you can begin to feel the openness where her thoughts come and go, where her emotions flow, where her body shines, and where her heart's desire abides. Practice feeling open as this place, where you and your lover feel the entire moment appearing now, and practice relaxing ever more deeply as this feeling-openness. Practice this now, and for the months and years of your life.

In every moment, freshly discover and open as the deepest place you can feel, in yourself and your lover.

Allow your depth of presence to freely emerge through your whole body, moment by moment. Practice breathing from your deep belly rather than your upper chest. Feel from your deep belly into your lover's body. Feel through your feet into the earth below and from your belly and heart into your lover and open your skull to the sky above, rather than limiting your awareness to the thoughts in your head and your lover's image in your eyes.

Moment by moment, throughout the day and while making love, feel all while feeling through all, opening as the depth of all. Practice feeling all with your whole-body sonar, feeling from your entire body—including your feet, belly, and chest—into your lover's body, sensing her tensions, her pleasures, breathing her rhythm, feeling her subtle changes of posture from head to toe.

If you attend mostly to your own thoughts and emotions, then your presence becomes trapped in your own head and body. You might *think* you are being present, but your lover can't feel it.

When you practice feeling the thoughts and emotions and body-energy of your lover—actually feeling into her, like you would feel into someone's muscles to massage open a knot, or feel into a room to most beautifully arrange the furniture—then your presence enlarges beyond your own surfaces. Your presence expands as far as your feeling-attention opens. If you can include your lover and the entire room in your open feeling-attention, then your presence is felt and honored by your lover and everyone else in the room.

When your lover feels your unambiguous and deep presence feeling into her, she can trust you. When she feels you feeling into her deep heart, she can open in resonance with your deep heart, the source of your integrity. When she feels you feeling open as the place of every moment, she can relax open as every moment's living light—including emotion, thought, and body.

As deep as the moment opens, you are feeling all and she is showing all. She feels you taking her and the entire moment into account, and deeply. She can trust the integrity of your direction and surrender fully alive as love-light, offering herself to be taken open by your unambiguous and deep presence.

In every relationship, there are decisions to be made and someone has to make them. Often it is best for both partners to decide and direct together. But sometimes the feminine partner finds it quite a relief when the masculine partner doesn't oblige her to make every decision and direct every course of action. Sometimes the feminine heart wants to relax, open, and shine as love while taken—surely and deeply—to the infinite place that every moment opens.

33

OPEN DEEPER
THAN NEED

∽

*In the midst of the
story of your life,
you can open now.*

The deepest desire of the feminine heart is to flow open with love. No matter how successful you are in your career, if you have a more feminine essence, then your heart will not feel fulfilled unless love is flowing in your life. Deep love. Trustable love. A love that allows you to surrender and relax open as love's graceful fullness.

You can feel how open you are to feminine fullness now. Is your womb full of soft delight? Are your inner thighs vibrant with life? Are your lips plump with love's kiss? If you are depressed, can you feel your darkness fully? Is your heart open, vulnerable, blossomed wide with the power of dark rain's storm? Are you breathing fully while ache saturates your heart and belly? If you are sexually aroused, can you show love's pleasure through your happy feet, your coy bellybutton, your spilled words of overflowing joy?

No matter how self-directed you have grown, your feminine heart blooms when filled with love. When your lover denies you love, then you feel hurt, and you close. Suppose your heart is wide open, ready to flow with love, but your lover is unwilling, maybe even aggressively unloving. Wounded by your lover's denial, your vulnerable heart cringes. Closing down, protecting itself, your heart hardens.

Your yearning is frustrated within the walls of pain's closure. Anger builds. You shout. You make demands. You express rage. And under it all, your heart hurts, wanting only to relax open as love. Behind most feminine anger is the deep yearning for love.

The masculine heart yearns not so much for love as for freedom. The masculine heart dreams not of swelling in fullness but of finally being free, liberated from constraints. One day, if you work hard enough, your burdens will diminish. You will have enough money to do what you want. You will figure out a grand theory and the problems will be solved. You will finish your projects and no longer be constrained by obligation. You will know enough, have enough, or succeed enough so you are no longer afraid of loss or failure.

In this moment, are you waiting for any achievement before you are willing to relax and open, exactly as you are? Is your work-life aiming for "one day" when you will finally be free to do what you really want to do? Do you ever get angry with your lover or children because you feel trapped by their need for attention?

When the masculine heart feels constrained by obligations—even the obligations of love—it begins to feel trapped. The loss of freedom irks the masculine heart. Even if you have chosen your career, family, and intimate relationship, you can still feel trapped by them. You begin to dream of what it would feel like to be free. Unbound.

Understand these different sources of anger: your feminine lover longs for love, your masculine lover longs for freedom. You can assuage your lover's anger by giving the feminine heart deep love, and by removing obligations from the masculine heart—even the demand for attention—so it can relax open in freedom. But being given what you need doesn't always spur you to open deeper than those needs.

Your needs—and your anger—can be signals to open more deeply. Why not open more deeply than your need for love or freedom right now? Because you are entangled in a life-story—a drama of needs—that seems necessary or at least significant.

The feminine heart is embroiled in the never-ending drama of love and its lack: Yes I am loved, no I am not loved, yes I am loved, no I am not loved …

The masculine heart is riveted by the illusion of working toward freedom: I am succeeding, I am failing, I am succeeding, I am failing…

You can offer temporary fulfillment to your lover—"Yes, I do love you" or "Yes, you are a great success"—but a few minutes later, the drama continues. If you have a more masculine essence, freedom is blissful, but the *struggle* for freedom makes you feel important. Working your way out of the trap gives your life meaning. With no problems to solve, you feel free for a while, and then you feel bored, useless, obsolete. The struggle for freedom makes your attention to life seem significant.

Even trivial challenges of constraint and breaking free seem to give your life a sense of purpose. Sitting alone you pick up a crossword puzzle. Resting at home you watch sports. You track the stock market. You feel trapped by life's dilemmas which resolution you seek. You relentlessly pursue financial success, artistic expression, social transformation, or spiritual liberation.

If you open as freedom now, your masculine adventure flashes as an unnecessary struggle, your need for significance evaporates. You are alive as spontaneous gifting. Each moment comes as it goes open. You, too. Open, and entirely given. Nothing remaining, but open, and entirely given.

And what happens when the *feminine* opens as love every now? Open as burgeoning love, birthed full as this moment, alive as all, who yearns to feel adored? Open as abundant love, who longs to feel cherished? Just as the masculine *needs* to feel trapped in order to feel a significant mission of importance, the feminine *needs* to feel unloved in order to take part in the heart-tugging drama of securing self-worth.

What is there to do if you are so full as love that more love isn't possible? If you truly trusted love abounding as all of life, then what would occupy your emotions? Unending and all-abundant love is the end of the feminine drama.

So, if you have a feminine essence, you will test love. Sabotage love. Deny love. You yearn to feel love withstanding your tests, rebounding from your sabotages, asserting itself through your denials. You want to feel your lover loving you even when you resist your lover. *Especially* when you resist. "You don't love me," you will say, only hoping your lover says, "Yes I do love you." "Leave me alone," you will say, as you close the door to your room, hoping that your lover enters. Abundant love isn't sufficient. It is love's *persistence* in the face of your *denial* that affords your valued pleasure. The feminine drama is about love *conquering* unlove.

A good love story requires that love be somehow threatened—perhaps by death, betrayal, denial, or tragic coincidence. In a fulfilling love story, love prevails. The feminine drama is about the triumph of love over loss, just as the masculine adventure is about breaking out of constraint into freedom. Love and freedom describe your true nature, but yearning and struggle describe the story of your life. It is a lie that sustains your place in time.

You may feel angry because your heart is hurt by unlove or trapped by life's obligations, but you can choose to go deeper than your life story, right now. You can use the energy of your anger to cut through the momentum and plunge to the heart of this moment. Rather than projecting blame and hope toward people and life—as if your relationships and plans can ever truly fulfill you—feel into the deepest desire of your heart, and obey your depth.

Feel your heart beating. Feel deeper than your beating heart, into love's depth. Feel so deep inside that you feel unendingly open. Really try doing this, now, even if you are angry, hurt, or frustrated. Whatever you feel in your heart, feel deeper, as deep as your feeling can feel.

As you feel into the unending open of depth, feel every single thing that occurs—your thoughts, your breath, the ground beneath your feet, the sky above you. Allow everything to flush the moment open with fragrance, memory, emotion, sensation, color, and sound. Feel open as the full moment, now.

Feel how long "now" lasts. Feel how long you are now. Feel as the entire now, as deep inside as you can, as far outward as you can, for as long as now opens. Feel every part of the entire moment, just as it is, as deep and wide as you can feel.

Relax open so you can feel open *as* this entire moment.

The love for which you long, the freedom for which you aim, is alive as you are open, now.

34

TRUST HIM MORE
than YOURSELF

∽◌∾

*For a woman to experience
her deepest sexual bliss and openness,
she must trust her lover's masculine
more than she trusts her own.*

Most women are capable of very deep sex. As a woman, your body and heart desire utter ravishment, total surrender, wave upon wave of pleasure and blissful love. But usually your sexual experience falls quite short of this.

If you are like most women, you know that sex can be better than it usually is. Even if you have not yet experienced it, you intuit a deeper sexual potential, although you may not know exactly how to get there.

For most women (and men), there are sexual skills to learn and emotional knots to untie. But no matter how skillful or easeful you become, your partner plays a huge role in how fully you will be willing to open sexually, physically, emotionally, and spiritually together.

Deep, ravishing sex involves the loving play of masculine and feminine forces. The masculine is consciousness, and manifests through the body as presence and direction. The feminine is love-light, and manifests through the body as radiance and life force. A sexy masculine person is very present and confident in direction. A sexy feminine person is very radiant and alive with life force. Presence and radiance attract each other and can realize their one-ness in the depth of sexual embrace.

In truth, masculine and feminine are aspects of the one conscious light that is called the divine by many names. For the fullest expression of sex, love is necessary but not sufficient. In order for sex to become sacred ravishment, conscious light plays as two: one partner embodies the masculine force of consciousness, presence, and purpose, while the other partner embodies the feminine force of love-light, radiance, and life force. These days, many men and women are afraid to sexually embody these divine expressions. Why?

Each person, every man and woman, has both masculine and feminine within them. Years ago, men were forced by social custom to always play the masculine role and women to play the feminine. This felt suppressive and limited. So, modern-day social custom has evolved to idealize balanced men and women: people who are each supposed to embody both masculine and feminine in a kind of psychological wholeness and relational independence.

Being whole unto oneself is a sign of psychological health. But being able to take the next step, to relinquish your boundaries in order to realize and express something larger than yourself, is a sign of spiritual maturity. To grow beyond mere self-sufficient wholeness, you and your lover can learn to open your boundaries and relinquish sexual autonomy for the sake of *two-bodied* divine play.

If you are sexually playing the feminine, you want to be swooned by your lover's unwavering presence, taken beyond all resistance into the overwhelming fullness of love, ravished into bliss. If you are playing the masculine, you want to feel your lover's trust and be attracted into your lover's radiant surrender so that you may give yourself utterly in the ravishment of your lover. As your hearts trust, your boundaries are relinquished, and masculine and feminine open—sometimes savagely, sometimes sublimely—as one conscious light.

But if you cling to psychological wholeness, you won't be willing to relinquish your boundaries of self-sufficiency. If you are like many modern women, you have worked hard to establish healthy boundaries and actualize your own direction and purpose; relinquishing your own navigation seems dangerous. Yet, if you have a more feminine sexual essence, this trust and sexual surrender is exactly what your deep heart desires. So, if you want to open in deep sexual play, you can practice trusting your lover to play the masculine while you play the feminine.

Even more difficult is the fact that, today, many women have a more highly developed masculine than their lovers do. You may not want to surrender to your lover's masculine direction because you don't trust it. And if your masculine direction is more evolved than your lover's is, then you *shouldn't* surrender to your lover's masculine. You are better off navigating yourself, following your own sexual lead! But if you do so, don't expect that your masculine lover will desire you for long.

Would you like to feel your masculine lover desiring and diving into your feminine radiance? Put another way, how attracted would you be if your lover *preferred* his own radiance to yours? Would it turn you on if he spent more time looking at himself in his dressing room mirror than at you, desiring himself and inspiring himself with his own beauty and shine?

Would that attract you sexually, if your masculine lover were "self-sufficiently radiant," so that he enjoyed his own shine more than yours? This is how you feel to him, if you are "self-sufficiently directional," trusting your own navigation more than his. Deep down, if you have a feminine sexual essence, then you want him to desire your radiance more than his own, and he wants you to desire his navigation more than your own. That is how the divine wants to make love through your bodies.

The truth is simple and stark: If you want to open sexually as the feminine divine, you won't experience the deepest bliss of *ravishment* unless you are with a lover who can sexually navigate deeper than you, and you *trust your lover's masculine more than your own.*

This is the bottom line. It doesn't matter how many sexual skills you know, or how open you are emotionally. If you don't trust your lover's masculine force and direction more than your own, you won't open completely. You won't let down your boundaries and surrender in deep trust to be sexually ravished by the divine masculine. Your lover's masculine consciousness, presence, and direction must be capable of bringing you to a deeper, more blissful and open love than you are capable of directing yourself, or you won't trust your lover's navigation. You won't open completely, and sex will stop short of divine ravishment.

Once you have balanced your inner masculine and feminine, once you have developed as an autonomous, whole person, then you have achieved psychological integration. But to experience divine *sexual* bliss, there is another step to take. Without losing your capacity for wholeness in everyday life, you can learn to relinquish your boundaries during sex, giving yourself entirely to be taken by the divine masculine force. But if your own masculine is more developed then your lover's, then you will stop short of utter surrender—and well you should! Why follow your lover's sexual navigation if your own is deeper and more heart-true?

Therefore, if you want to experience the fullest divine play as the feminine sexual partner, then you must choose a lover worthy of your trust. If you are in a relationship, your lover can cultivate his whole-body depth of presence as you cultivate your capacity to receive his heart-true navigation. Specifically, your lover's masculine consciousness, presence, and direction should be more developed than yours, more capable of taking you into utter sexual openness and spiritual surrender than you are capable of taking yourself.

If your lover can offer you this gift, then why not let go of your own sexual lead and surrender to ravishment as you have always yearned?

If you don't trust your lover's masculine direction more than yours, then the best you can hope for is love without deep ravishment. If love is all you want, then the play of masculine and feminine is irrelevant. You can enjoy love with your friends, children, and parents. You can love yourself. You can love the divine. You can love your intimate partner in many ways, cuddling, gardening, raising a family. Love is the very nature of your being, the very nature of all being. Love is the openness of every moment.

But if you find yourself yearning for a love that includes *ravishing* sexual play, if you want to be taken, swept off your feet, and overwhelmed by the unrelenting force of divine masculine presence, then you must be with a lover whose masculine direction you trust—and desire—more than your own. Only then will you allow yourself to surrender, receive, and bloom open wide as the moment's full light of love.

35

EXAGGERATE SEX TO LIBERATE LOVE

∽

*Stretching your limits
frees your natural radiance
and native presence.*

Imagine the most delicious, full, abandoned sexual loving you can. Not just pleasurable sex, and not just loving sex, but the kind of sex that leaves you *ruined* in love. You are opened, flayed, undone. You are helplessly taken, eaten by your lover, crushed by love's weight. You give everything, you love your lover to death, you "kill" your lover softly in love, who has given you their heart, unprotected, wanting, begging to be taken.

Together, you open so entire that no part remains unsoaked as love. Your bodies saturate as light, your minds undo deep-water clear, your sensations flame the entire moment open—and yet your loving continues, hot, wet, alive.

How do you practice this kind of sexual ravishment if you don't yet trust your masculine lover's navigation to love's depth, or you don't yet receive your feminine lover's full-bodied, pleasure-saturated, open surrender?

If you are the feminine partner in a relationship, exaggerate your gift of love-light to entice your masculine lover's deeper presence. The fullness of your love-delight and the depth of his loving presence go deeper together.

They are the two sides of each sexual moment—light and consciousness merging through two bodies to open as one conscious light.

The feminine is alive as love-light, and your feminine body is the field of your masculine partner's delight. He loves to see your body ripe with life, full with pleasure, alive with love. He loves to feel your body let go and open to him, as light does to consciousness, to receive his presence deeply. He wants to enter you and fill you and pervade you to heart-blooming love-death, but he is only invited in as deeply as you trust. The more your body opens and displays love's pleasure, the more your masculine partner is drawn to dive into your heart-light, taking you even deeper than you would go alone.

The shallower your body's pleasure is, the shallower your lover's presence will be. If you want your lover to *take* you to love's depth with absolute integrity and fully present navigation, offer him your open and trusting body of delight. Enlarge these sexual gifts to enlarge his conscious presence with you.

If your pleasure makes you want to moan a bit, magnify your offering. Moan so loud, writhe with so much abandon, that your body swallows your lover like a wild sea of pleasure bucking and swirling beneath his boat. Force him to navigate with more presence by offering him your unkempt gifts of pleasure.

Smile "yes" when he navigates you into deeper waters. Pause for a moment to remind him to come to presence if he gets lost in his own pleasure, or in yours. As he learns to remain present, exaggerate your showing. If he kisses your neck with fully conscious passion, receive pleasure so deeply it reverberates through all of you, your body quaking with life-force, your lips mouthing for love, your pelvis reaching to be filled.

Your feminine sexual gift is to offer yourself as love-light to be taken and pervaded by consciousness. Show yourself, through your entire body, as light wanting to be taken, seen, felt, pervaded, shot through, ravished, murdered by love, as every moment is.

Enlarge your showing by magnifying the display of your sexual pleasure, always offering from your deepest heart. As a feminine sexual art, practice offering light's body, wet, gaping, hungry, as open to be seen and felt as this moment is alive. Scream more loudly, undulate more fully, give your pleasure to be felt by your lover like the moment gives light to be seen—open wide as full-blown life. This is the feminine practice.

If you are the masculine partner, practice the heart-precision of conscious feeling, touching without grasping, tasting without drooling. Like a surfer on a wave, without sticking in one place too long, feel every nuance of your lover's energy, her breath, her movements, her shivers, tensions, and whispers—and lovingly take her to the beach of openness beyond this moment's edge.

Like a soldier, your senses acute and open wide, feel into her unseen parts with heightened sensitivity, flushing her closed thickets with the conscious fire of your breath and loins, moving deeper into her love inch by inch, as she receives your tender surveillance.

If you feel a part of your lover unopen, inhale her tension, warm it with the heat of your love-desire, and fill her with your outward thrust of gentle open-ness. Breathe her entire body as if it were yours. Breathe her body to open, moment by moment, kiss by kiss, thrust by thrust. Stay with her, sometimes still, sometimes savage, feeling into her deepest heart, as she opens and closes in waves that test your navigation. Feel into her heart even while her pleasure bucks and throes. Feel through your own pleasure into her openness, even while your flesh singes.

As she goes open more wildly, penetrate her to deeper love. Force her to open as love beyond pleasure, gently, caringly, with utter feeling-merger, breathing her heart. No matter how hard or soft your bodies writhe and roll, stay tender at heart, open to depth, yours and hers. Persist. Feelingly persist.

Your capacity to navigate with integrity depends on your strength of depth. Your attention may wander to attractive surface features: breasts, lips, ass. Dive into her luscious radiance through her offered portals of attraction. Like a feeling-sonar, sound out her heart and breathe her endless openness, deeper than the surface moves. Persist feeling open as love's depth while also enjoying her offered sparkles, ripples, nipples, and shine.

You are dying. She is dying. Feel death as you open, at one with your lover's heart. As you love more than you have ever loved, feel all dying.

This entire moment is full-blush born and instantly gone—you and her with it. Feel the entire moment—including you and your lover—appearing to nothing but light's open.

Love each other to death and emerge renewed now. Together, love open as conscious light.

The masculine partner breathes open his lover, warming her closure to soft surrender with his gentle and persistent force of presence. The feminine partner offers her untamed light as a portal for her lover's entry, attracting his wandering attention with her feast of delight, calling him to depth with the surrender of her heart.

If your lover drifts or closes, beckon your lover's heart with humor. With a tickle, a beep, or a funny face, loosen the moment to open, and continue deepening the offer of your sexual loving, moment by moment, year by year.

36

HOLD
NOTHING BACK

～

*A woman often won't tell
her man directly how
much she appreciates his gifts.*

A man sometimes goes to great lengths to gift his woman. He works hard for her, creates art, purchases exquisite gems for her, and helps her to grow. But if he waits for his woman's acknowledgment, he suffers. A woman can't express her appreciation fully to a man who needs to feel appreciated.

A woman wants to feel that her man is not dependent on her. She wants to feel that her man wants her, desires her, but does not *need* her. A needy man is a turn-off. A man who needs to be acknowledged for his giving ruins the gift.

Of course, all men are needy to some extent. And to grow into integrated selfhood requires that men learn to express their needs clearly. But to grow beyond personal integration and truly open fully, a man can learn that his life is a full-blown sacrifice. A life well lived is a life wherein your gifts are given fully, no holding back—even if you are not appreciated, acknowledged, or noticed for the giving.

Most women want a man with this kind of offering-strength, a man who does not need her pat on the back to continue giving his gifts to the world or to her. He is dedicated to giving his gifts in spite of resistance by the world or by her. A woman loves to feel that even when she doesn't acknowledge her man, he continues on his path without collapse. Then she can trust him. His needs, and therefore her moods, do not sag his life.

If you are a man, notice how much acknowledgment you want from your woman or the world for your gifts. Every man wants to be appreciated for what he gives, but your gifts need not wilt when they are seemingly unnoticed. You can learn to give your gifts fully, without holding back while you wait for adequate acknowledgment—which rarely comes as fully as you hope, especially when you need it most.

As you grow, you realize that your woman's lack of acknowledgment acts as a test. Are you giving like an artist who must express art, a saint who must offer compassion, a father who must provide his children with the best upbringing he can, regardless of how much appreciation he gets for it? When you die, will you know that you have given yourself utterly to the world, to your woman, to your family, holding nothing back? Or are you still like a little boy eagerly performing for the sake of mom's applause? Very little helps you mature beyond neediness more than the appreciation you want from your woman, but don't get.

37

OFFER SEX FOR
THE SAKE OF ALL

~∞~

In intimate relationships,
transcending conflict often
requires giving what you most
want to hold back.

When you and your lover are feeling separated by conflict, how can you shift the energy from tension to passion? If your lover is a man, grab his genitals. If your lover is a woman, be totally present with tender gazes, loving words, and affectionate touch.

A man's body is built so that first comes sexual flow, then emotional openness. For most men, overtly sexual touch quickly opens their heart when it is closed. But a woman's body is built so that first comes emotional openness, then sexual flow. That is, most women don't want to open sexually until they are first open emotionally.

For masculine-essence men, energy opening comes first, then emotional opening. Such a man often needs to feel pleasurable, sexual energy flowing—his woman's hair against his groin, her lips on his neck, her nipples brushing his thigh—before he is relaxed and attracted into life enough to want to open emotionally. The masculine is not at home in life and body, and therefore must first be attracted into the flesh before being willing and able to commune through the heart.

For feminine-essence women, emotional opening comes first, then energy flows. Such a woman wants to feel her man's presence, his caring, his heart connecting with hers, and *then* she opens in the flow of sexual energy. When a woman is tense and closed, her man would be making a mistake to abruptly grab her breasts. She would feel angry, even more closed, perhaps even disgusted at his insensitive grope.

On the other hand, when a man is tense and closed, his woman would be surprised at how quickly his heart opens when he feels her lips around his penis—the more abrupt and sudden the better. A man's heart openness follows his body's flow of energy, whereas a woman's flow of sexual energy follows her heart openness.

In intimacy with your opposite-essence lover, the doorway to openness is often exactly what you don't want to do. Deep intimacy requires that you know how to open a sexual essence quite unlike yours.

The key to opening a man's heart is to understand that, in intimacy, the masculine essence usually values the gift of life-energy more than the gift of emotional presence. Life-energy—expressed sexually and as bodily radiance—is so valued that many men have left a woman they deeply love for a woman with whom they can flow more deeply in sexual passion. People's hearts are attracted to open by their reciprocal. Masculine *consciousness* is attracted to feminine *energy*. A consciously *present* woman is great, but a gloriously *radiant* woman makes a man happy to be alive.

A radiant woman, on the other hand, yearns for depth of *presence* in intimacy. She wants a man who can truly feel her, a man who can feel through her surfaces into her deep heart. She doesn't want a man who is distracted, ambiguous, and all over the place. A *radiant* man is great, but a man who is truly *present* provides the feminine with an opportunity to trust, open, and know she is taken into account. She can feel her man's deep integrity and strength of consciousness.

In intimacy, most men are attracted to open with a lover's radiance and into-the-body-inviting energy. Most women are attracted to open with a lover's depth of feeling and strength of conscious presence. This is true while making love and also in the middle of an intimate conflict.

When your lover hurts you, it is common to punish your lover by with-holding your gifts. When feeling jilted, women close down sexually and cease to offer radiance. Men pull away and cease to offer presence. Over time, a woman's dark closure or a man's distant avoidance can sever the flow of passion. To re-create an arc of attraction in your relationship, to evoke your lover's desire to open with you heart-to-heart, practice offering the gifts of your sexual essence. Offer radiance as a gift to presence, presence as a gift to radiance.

If your lover is a masculine-essence man, erotically shock his body into full energy-flow, using your radiant body to sexually arouse, inspire, and magne-tize his, and *then* commune with his heart through gaze, touch, and words. If your lover is a feminine-essence woman, feel into her deeply, communicating your fully present love through gaze, touch, and words *first*, communing with her heart in sweet merger until she begs for sexual contact.

An unexpected poem or bouquet of flowers can open a woman like unex-pected oral sex can open a man. "Have I ever told you how much I deeply love you?" can open a woman as much as, "Have I ever told you how much I love to hold you in my mouth?" can open a man. At heart, all men and woman desire to open in profound love. But the body has its locks and keys. The closed feminine body opens in response to loving *presence:* deep feeling and full emotional connection. The closed masculine body opens in response to loving *energy:* deep radiance and sudden sexual delight.

First you practice opening and loving yourself. Then you can expand the gifts of your loving. You can practice opening with your lover, skillfully giving and receiving the gifts of presence and radiance, serving each other to open even more than you might on your own. Eventually, as you open beyond your own closure with the help of your lover's gifts, you can begin practicing to open as the entire living moment.

As you open beyond yourself, you begin to feel the suffering of all, and you are naturally moved to help all, to love all, to open as all. It hurts to do less. Any closure that you feel in the moment—yours or someone else's—you are moved to feel, breathe, and open. Opening to give and receive love with your lover during times of closure can be a rehearsal for opening to give and receive love open as the entire moment.

As a woman, when you receive your man's deep presence and open to him, don't stop there. Open to receive all. Open *as* all. Allow your man's presence to be like a wedge that opens your body and heart to receive the presence of the entire moment. Breathe in your man, breathe everyone, breathe the entire moment, deeply into your heart, offering yourself open to be taken by all, receiving and opening to infinity, radiating love from your heart, open alive as all.

As a man, when your attention is drawn to the gift of pleasurable energy that your woman's body gives you, don't stop there. As you breathe more fully—opened out by your woman's loving ministrations—open to feel the radiant touch of the entire moment. Breathe open to feel the shifting colors, sounds, and motions of all, far and near. Allow your lover's sexual invitation to draw you into opening, feeling, and entering the energy of the entire living moment. Feeling outward into all and through all, open as all to infinity.

Through your lover's gifts, open to make love as the entire moment.

When serving your lover, offer your gifts of deep presence and pleasurable energy so that your lover may open as the entire moment, for the sake of all.

38

AWAKEN SEXUALLY
AS BLISS AND EMPTINESS

∽

Sooner or later, even sex
with someone you love
can become a routine.

Sex seems to promise so much. Skin aflame with unbearable bliss. Sobbing embraces of vulnerable rapture. Transcendent merger as utter oneness. But usually, sex is fairly mundane.

Men get hard, pump and grunt, squirt out their tension, and relax. Women get wet, moan and hump, seize and weep, and snuggle in warm comfort. At first exciting, sex can become quite predictable. Even good sex can become standardized.

In this way, sex is like the rest of life. It's actually less than you hoped. For almost everyone who reaches middle age, sex and life become a customary enjoyment, a habitualized routine of pleasure, comfort, and pain that is consoling at best, and often meaningless.

This is good. Meaninglessness is a sign of growth. When something becomes boring it means you are ready to go deeper. When you are humping away but still unsatisfied, you are ready for deeper sex.

Sex that feels empty reveals a deeper truth: Sex *is* empty. Just like any other moment of life.

When you allow yourself to feel sex completely, you feel two things. On the one hand, your genitals are engorged, your chest is heaving, and your passions are inflamed. On the other hand, so what? You've been there before and nothing fundamental has resulted. This moment of sex—like every moment—is amazingly rich and deliciously textured, but also strangely vacant.

Eventually you realize that nothing specific is missing from your sexual life. You can certainly improve your sexual skills—communicating your emotions more fully and enjoying multiple orgasms that last for hours—yet, when your fascination with new pleasure and achievement wears off, you become re-aware of a haunting sense of emptiness.

The truth is, every sexual moment is empty. *Every* moment is empty, insubstantial, unreal. And every moment is full, tangible, explosively alive. Like a vivid dream, each moment is intensely impactful, spontaneously dynamic, and instantly gone, as if it never occurred. Sex can be tender, a miracle of love, yet vaporously inconsequential, a wistful *deja vu*. Simultaneously, sex is intense and vanished; even when utterly blissful, it is also utterly empty.

Naive youth gets lost in the brief rush of pleasure. Depressed grown-ups linger in the not-enough of vacant embrace. The truth is that every moment is tangibly insubstantial. The true lover surrenders beyond all hold, as naked life *is*.

But to get to this point requires outgrowing your grasp on feeling good—or bad—about sex. Early in your sexual life, enjoy the thrill of romance and fascination for as long as it lasts. Then, frolic in the middle days of unsatisfying but decent sexual routine.

Eventually, when hope has worn away, when you have no other choice, relax in the coat of emptiness you already wear. Don love's open bliss. Bear edgeless luminosity. Sex is a revelation of what *is*, intensely.

39

BE ALIVE
AS GIFTING

〜

People less open than you
can be frustrating;
those more open than you
can be offensive.

Openness is valuable. Others feel your masculine openness as strong presence. Your intentions are clear and your attention is tangible. People can trust you. Feeling your unwavering integrity, they offer you their business. Feeling your unperturbable virtue, they offer you their confidence. The trustable force of your presence is valuable to them.

Feminine openness is felt as radiance. When your body and heart are open, life force flows through you unimpeded. Your eyes shine. Your hips move like the ocean. Your voice sings with the force of nature. People are blessed just to see you, to imbibe your glorious fullness. Your brightness fills the room. Your smile awakens the hearts of those around you. The gift of your radiance is priceless.

At depth, your openness is the same as everyone's openness. Still, you can feel when closure occurs—you can feel when someone is being more uptight than you. They seem agitated, closed, dark, tense, and humorless. Naturally, you want to help such a person. But after a while, they can drain you. When you are with someone who is more *closed* than you are being, then your energy flows to him or her.

When you are with someone who is more *open* than you are being, his or her energy flows to you. You feel inspired by their grace, awed by their clarity. Eventually, their force of character may seem to influence you so much that you can become suspicious. If you aren't able to admit their superior openness, then you must find another justification for their influence on you. Suddenly, they may seem to be controlling you, belittling you, using you. You begin to hate them, even though you are also benefiting from their gifts.

In any moment that someone is more open than you, they are more present or radiant than you. Compared to you, they are more clear, effective, insightful, sexy, mysterious, beautiful, or powerful. Even though this person also has their share of weaknesses, the force of their presence or radiance still pours *from* them *to* you. You can actually feel their energy, force, or power influencing you.

You can receive this energy for your benefit. You can offer gratitude and appreciation to your superior friend. You can receive their gifts and perhaps grow into their peer, sharing the same depth of openness, passing on your own gifts of presence and radiance to those more closed than you.

Or, if you don't like to feel yourself as inferior, then you will end up denying your superior friend's energy through resistance, asserting your independence and equality, while secretly envious of their brilliance and glory.

You may feel afraid to speak up in their presence. You may feel jealous of their awesome beauty, desiring to be like them even while you take solace in pronouncing their flaws. You may find yourself exaggerating their weaknesses so that you can feel less inferior, even though you know that your presence is weaker or your radiance is more faint than theirs. Knowing your inferiority—feeling your dim bulb almost invisible in the shine of their sun—can be very offensive to your need for self-worth.

At depth, all people are equal. All people are equally divine, alive as conscious light. For most people, however, consciousness becomes degraded as their attention remains trapped in the drama of their everyday struggle with money, relationships, and health. Their presence becomes absorbed in life's toil. Thus, a really present person, a person whose consciousness fills the room with a tangible force, is rather rare.

The shine of most people's heart, the natural light of their being, gets obscured by their bodily tension and the stress of their lives. The fresh radiance of a young lover eventually gets clouded and dimmed by years of betrayal, loss, and fear. By middle age, your shining heart may be encased in so many layers of mistrust and protection that your face seems shrouded in gauze of darkness. It is rare to meet an adult whose natural radiance still brightens a room with energy and love.

Although all people, at heart, are equal as conscious light, each person expresses a different degree of presence and radiance, depending on how open they are in the moment. Sometimes, after years of suffering, a person can develop habits of closure that are not so easy to release. Their closure serves as a kind of protection against further hurt and also obscures their would-be gifts of consciousness and light.

If your true gifts have become lost in the struggle with life's demands, then you are in pain. Ungiven gifts hurt. Unoffered love sears the heart. Unexpressed insight sucks the strength from your bones. When you meet a person of greater openness, your closure stands in stark relief. Feeling the choices you have made of security and self-guardedness, acutely aware of your yearning heart, lost time, and ungiven gifts, you can either surrender open and receive the force of superior openness or fortify your closure.

When you meet a superior man or woman, your only real choices are to open fully and receive their gifts or to crucify them and be relieved of their force. To grow, you must learn to absorb their intensity of openness that would otherwise simply make you feel how crimped you are.

Just as water always flows downhill, so do presence and radiance. In the company of a really open man or woman, their force will naturally impinge on you, exposing your fearfully limited stance in life, threatening your self-worth, offering the power necessary to awaken your heart into fullness. But you must be willing to feel your heart's wounds and terrors or else you will close and protect yourself, striking back at the source of openness you most yearn to become.

Your gifts of attention and energy, of presence and radiance, are always flowing from you to those who are more clenched than you in the moment. And you are constantly inspired and gifted by those who are more open than you in the moment. The gift must be given. Circulation is the law. If you try to hold back, you suffer. You must freely *give* your deepest gifts without holding back, and you must also freely *receive* from the source upstream.

Suffering is only your refusal to open. You are alive as gifting.

EPILOGUE: BLUE TRUTH
An Excerpt from *Wild Nights*

Mykonos nodded toward the stage where a band was supposed to play later in the afternoon. From a door near the stage the waitress came and made her way toward our table. She was gorgeous. Her hips were wrapped in a purple sarong. Her breasts were held by a small yellow bikini top. Her athletic belly was golden-brown from hot hours in the sun. In the long braid of her blond hair were two bright hibiscus flowers, one yellow, one red.

"Yes," Mykonos said languidly, hissing the final "s" as he usually did when talking about women or God. "Yesss. She is beautiful, is she not?"

We all nodded, in our own way. Lemuel gave his usual slack-jawed, "Uh-huh." Dimitri—who told us he had gone home the previous night when he felt hurt by Michelle's affections toward Mykonos—was more interested in the fish tacos on his plate than the waitress, though he looked up and exclaimed an enthusiastic, "Oh yeah!"

Paco, however, definitely seemed to be in some kind of mood. He stood up from our table, shaking his head and mumbling something to himself, and went to play some beach volleyball not far from where we were sitting.

I couldn't keep my eyes off of the waitress. She seemed perfect. Absolutely beautiful. I wanted her.

"Breathe her in, my friend," Mykonos said softly, "She is all around you."

My attention snapped from the waitress as if from a dream. *She is all around you.* Mykonos had a way of waking me up.

"Mm-hmm. You like her, don't you?" Mykonos asked me.

"Yes."

"You want her."

"Yes."

"Look around. So does everybody else."

I looked around. There were red-faced tourists talking about the scenery and chewing their food. Paco was playing volleyball with a group of young locals on the beach. A few couples sat at tables around us, holding hands, sipping their drinks from huge ice-filled glasses and speaking to each other in voices of quiet affection.

Nobody seemed to notice the waitress, who had stopped at the table right next to ours to take an order. She was in her early twenties, probably a college student or a surfer who was making some extra money for the summer, waitressing at this beachside café and bar. Her skin was flawless and her nipples pressed their shape deep into my brain.

"Yesss," Mykonos continued, as if speaking to himself, "Everybody wants her."

Then the waitress came to our table. She was stunning. She was standing so close I could see the fine blonde hairs on her tummy. Her eyes were clear and blue, and her smile was truly happy, as if she was having the time of her life waiting tables. The slit of her sarong revealed lotion-glistening thighs all the way up to the yellow bikini bottom she wore under her silky wrap.

"Hello, my dear," Mykonos said to the waitress, "We'll have three pitchers of beer and some more fish tacos for Dimitri," nodding toward our friend who looked up from his plate and smiled.

"Is that all?" asked the waitress.

"That's it for now," Mykonos answered.

As she walked away, I watched her until she disappeared through the door next to the stage.

"Poor Paco," Mykonos said, gazing out toward the beach where the volleyball game was in progress. "He thinks he can play. Look at him. He thinks he's really good."

Paco was a lot better at volleyball than I was, and as far as I knew, he was a lot better than Mykonos, too.

"All puffed up, thinking he looks so good. One day, Paco is going to find his heart. And then…" Mykonos trailed off, smiling as if he knew the punchline to a joke that was yet to come.

When a busboy brought our beer, Mykonos filled his glass and raised it. "To the Great One."

"To the Great One," we all joined in, raising our beer, and then drinking.

I kept looking for the waitress.

We drank beer, snacked a bit, and relaxed, as the afternoon grew long. Paco finally finished playing and returned to our table. Mykonos greeted him.

"You're a fine player, Paco."

"Yeah, I'm not bad. Used to be better. I used to play in college and…"

"Would you like a beer, my friend," Mykonos interrupted.

"Sure," Paco answered, as Lemuel filled his glass.

"To the Great One," Paco toasted, raising his glass.

We all raised our glasses, and drank.

"We are all enjoying this fine day together, filled with love, and our friend here has his mind on a whoor," Mykonos said toward me with a raise of his eyebrow. He said the word "whoor" like it rhymed with "tour" whenever he was praising a woman for her radiance, her light, her open-heartedness. For Mykonos, "whoor" meant something very different than the common word "whore." A "whoor" was a vision of light, a goddess.

"Where is she now?" Mykonos asked me, looking directly into my eyes. His eyes were very dark, the deep black of an endless well.

"I don't know. Probably back in the kitchen, I guess."

"You can't feel her now? Hmmm? Are you *bereft* of woman?" He emphasized the word "bereft" to tease me; it was the kind of word I would use, not he.

"No. I'm not *bereft* of women."

"I said *woman*, not women."

I looked into his eyes. He held my gaze without moving. Suddenly, everything stopped. It was as if we were in a movie, and everything froze motionless—the people, the birds, the ocean, all completely still—while Mykonos continued.

"Breathe her."

I couldn't tell if Mykonos said this out loud, or if I was remembering something he had said earlier. I noticed that I had stopped breathing. I began to breathe again. Still, nothing else moved. As I inhaled, a fragrance filled my body with tendrils of love, curling like paisleys deep in my heart. Mykonos held my gaze with his deep black eyes. The bliss of paisley was now almost too much to bear.

And everybody was laughing and talking suddenly, the birds flew and the ocean lapped up on the beach, as Mykonos broke his gaze and reached for his beer.

"Do you think she likes you?" he asked me.

"I don't know."

"She doesn't even know you exist," Mykonos said. "Lemuel, how long has your friend here been obsessed with women?"

"I never thought he was obsessed with women," Lemuel answered.

"Oh, yes. He is obsessed with women, although he doesn't like them."

"He seems to like women to me."

"Not exactly," Mykonos said while pulling back his lips, exposing his crooked teeth. "Do you know what I'm talking about, Dimitri? No, you do not. Look at Dimitri eating. Look at how happy he is."

Mykonos laughed and drank more beer. As usual, I tried to keep up with Mykonos, drinking whenever he did, gulp for gulp. I felt a little woozy. The air was still hot, though it was getting late.

The band climbed up on the stage and began playing. It was typical bar brand music, generic and uninteresting.

"Yes! Right on!" Mykonos began shouting to the band.

I was still thinking about what Mykonos had said to Lemuel. What did he mean that I didn't like women?

"C'mon men," Mykonos said to us. "Let's give the band some energy. They are here to serve us and bring us happiness. Show them you are into it."

"But Mykonos, I'm not into it," Paco said as he read the back of the menu.

"Paco, you're not *into* anything. Have another beer, my friend." Mykonos refilled his glass.

Paco continued. "I mean it. I don't want to fake it. This music sucks."

Mykonos smiled wide and shook his head in mock disbelief.

He pushed his craggy face forward so his bent nose was inches from Paco's. "This is God," Mykonos said. He paused for a moment, smiling into Paco's face, and then sat back, bursting out with laughter.

"Who the hell am I hanging out with? A mutant, a reject from Shaker Heights, a dolphin, and the Lord of Darkness himself! You guys are unbelievable! This is it! Right now! This is the Divine Vision! It doesn't get more divine than this!"

Mykonos raised his glass high. This time, he didn't say a toast. He touched the air with his beer glass, toasting silently with an unseen guest.

"I don't know. Maybe it's time to go home." Mykonos wondered out loud.

Dimitri chimed in. "We can give the band energy. Alright!" he shouted to the band. "Alright! We love you!"

I cringed. I couldn't believe how naïve and gullible Dimitri seemed.

"Yes!" Mykonos yelled right along with Dimitri. "We're with you!"

The band looked up directly at our table. They smiled and nodded. Mykonos lifted his beer to them, and smiled. "Good job Dimitri."

Paco continued to sulk. He hunched his shoulders and pressed his lips together.

"What's wrong, Paco? You can play volleyball with great energy, but you can't give love to the band?" Mykonos asked.

"But I don't love them. I don't even know them!"

"Ahh. Paco." Mykonos pulled back his lips again and hissed. "Yesss. You don't know them. You can only love. That's all you can *ever* do, Paco. The band is always playing, whether you like them or not. Do you know what I mean? The lady is always showing herself to you, whether you like her or not"—I knew Mykonos was talking to me now—"and all you can do is love. Even if the band doesn't know who you are. Even if the lady doesn't care."

"She's a beautiful whoor, is she not?" Mykonos asked, looking directly into my eyes. I began to feel like I was sinking, being pressed down at my heart into a hole with no bottom, spinning a little, and suddenly the waitress was at our table, refilling our water glasses. She must have come up from behind me.

"Are you having a good day?" Mykonos asked the waitress.

"Yes. It's a little busy. But I like it that way."

"My friend here finds you beautiful," Mykonos said, nodding toward me. I couldn't believe Mykonos had said that.

"Thank you," the waitress said, without a hint of shyness. I thought she must receive compliments all the time.

"It's a beautiful day, isn't it?" Mykonos asked her.

"Really beautiful. I love clear, sunny days."

"You can feel the sunshine in your heart, can't you?"

She stopped filling our glasses and looked at Mykonos for the first time.

"Yes. I guess I can."

"Your heart is very bright, my dear." Mykonos continued, his deep black eyes looking into hers.

She smiled and held gaze with Mykonos. Nobody said a word. Finally, she looked down, swallowed, looked up again at Mykonos, breathed deeply, nodded, and walked off.

"A truly fine whoor, that one."

Everyone lifted their glasses and drank with Mykonos, except Paco.

"Do you have a problem, Paco?" Mykonos asked.

"No."

"Does he have a problem?" Mykonos asked, turning to me.

"Paco doesn't like to be happy."

"That's not true," Paco quickly responded, leaning forward and crinkling his forehead. "I just don't like to lie."

"You think we are lying, is that it, Paco?" Mykonos asked.

"Well, sort of. I mean, you don't even know that waitress, but you treat her like a princess. The band sucks, but you pretend that it's good. I just don't feel like faking it."

"Paco, Paco, Paco," Mykonos said through his teeth. "Why the hell are you alive?"

"I don't know. Maybe I shouldn't be."

"Paco, I think Mykonos is asking why *anyone* is alive," Lemuel suggested.

"Yesss. What does 'alive' mean?"

"I don't know." Paco said, with a shrug.

"Well, what does being alive *feel* like?" Mykonos asked.

"Right now, pretty bad. I feel like you guys are attacking me."

"Paco, look at these strange friends of yours here. They love you. You know it."

"Yeah. I guess so. I just don't want to pretend I'm happy if I'm not. I don't want to pretend that I like the band if I don't."

"Why not?" Mykonos asked as he drank his beer.

"Because I want to be authentic."

Mykonos laughed so suddenly that he spewed beer over Lemuel. Lemuel took off his spotted glasses and wiped them clean with a napkin, smiling.

"Paco," Mykonos continued, "look around you."

Paco straightened his spine and looked around. "Yeah?"

"What do you see?"

"The ocean, the sky, the sand, a bunch of people."

"And what are they doing?"

"I don't know. Whatever they are doing."

"Exactly." Mykonos sat back and swallowed another gulp of cold beer. His gaze was now directed over the ocean, as if he were looking at something far, far away, perhaps just over the horizon. "Volleyball. Women. Fish tacos. You've got to feel her right now, all around you like the colors of a flame, touching you always. Do you know what I mean? You've got to love her, breathe her, feel the truth of her, until she dies. What else are you going to do?"

"That might work for you, but not for me," Paco announced sitting back in his chair.

Mykonos paused and breathed deeply. He put his hand on Paco's thigh and spoke lovingly, "You are not alive for yourself, my friend. You are not here to play volleyball and withhold your love because you don't feel it. You are *alive* as love. This whole place is lit up as love. If you can't feel it, don't punish others for your inability to feel. Loosen up, my friend. Feel the mystery of you and this whole place, breathe the mystery—and then you tell me if this place is other than love. Hmmm? Maybe *you* are living a lie, Paco, not me. Love is the truth—of you and all these other monkeys."

"But I don't *feel* love," Paco said, almost pleading.

"Ahh, yesss." Mykonos sat still for a few minutes, looking far off toward the horizon. Suddenly he smiled hugely, and started to speak with moist eyes. "Have you ever looked closely at a flame, Paco? The reds and yellows are easy to see, but deep in the center of the flame is blue. You can easily avoid the blue, miss it altogether if you just look at the surface colors. But always blue is here, deeper than where your vision stops. Even now, blue." Quietly, Mykonos made a sound I could barely hear, and then sat in silence, still gazing far away.

After a few moments, Mykonos pointed. "Look into the sky. Look deeply. Blue. Look into the ocean. The deeper the water, the bluer it gets. Blue is the color of deep. And beyond everything you can see, deeper than all the things you like or don't like, there is a place where everything is blue, so blue, like water that does not end…" Mykonos stopped himself and smiled.

"I still don't see why I should try to give people love if I don't feel love," said Paco.

"Because, my dear friend, you *are* love. But you are trapped in the colors that possess your eyes and curl around your heart. Feel deeper than your sulk, feel deeper than what you can see, feel into the blue. The waitress, fish tacos, volleyball—everything you can see and know is more shallow than the blue truth."

"And just what is the blue truth, Mykonos?" asked Paco.

"For you, Paco? What is the true blue truth? Whatever sets your heart free. Whatever allows you to feel deeper than things seem. If you want to curl up and pout, Paco, nobody can stop you. But it hurts you and everyone to do so, because it's a lie, and deep down, you know it."

Mykonos turned again to the band. "Yes!" he shouted as the lead singer hit a high note, "Yes! Right on!"

The lead singer looked at Mykonos and smiled. The band began to play with more life. The whole place seemed to come alive, to get brighter.

"Can you feel her now?" Mykonos suddenly turned and asked while gazing deep into my eyes. "Can you feel her alive as everything, or do you still only feel her when she fills your damn glass?" he asked me.

"I feel her, Mykonos."

"Yesss. When you are ready, when you embrace her for the sake of the truth of her, you'll know who she really is. Now you only see the tip of her flame, pulling you in and burning you up in all this surface loving, in all these bodies

Blue Truth

and eating and sexing. She's fantastic! My friends, if you could see her surrendered over, *totally* taken by the Great One where no appearance burns at all, where it is cooler even than blue ... "

Mykonos smiled and showed his teeth. He reached for his beer, looked at each of us, and laughed. "Perhaps, for now, the blue truth is enough. Hmmm?"

DAVID DEIDA RESOURCES

BOOKS

The Way of the Superior Man
A Spiritual Guide to Mastering the Challenges of Women, Work, and Sexual Desire

David Deida explores the most important issues in men's lives—from career and family to women and intimacy to love and sex—to offer the ultimate spiritual guide for men living a life of integrity, authenticity, and freedom.

ISBN: 978-1-59179-257-4 / U.S. $17.95

Dear Lover
A Woman's Guide to Men, Sex, and Love's Deepest Bliss

How do you attract and keep a man capable of meeting what you most passionately yearn for? To answer this question, David Deida explores every aspect of the feminine practice of spiritual intimacy, from sexuality and lovemaking to family and career to emotions, trust, and commitment.

ISBN: 978-1-59179-260-4 / U.S. $16.95

Intimate Communion
Awakening Your Sexual Essence

David Deida's first book lays the foundation for his teaching on the integration of intimacy and authentic spiritual practice.

Finding God Through Sex
Awakening the One of Spirit Through the Two of Flesh

No matter how much we pray or meditate, it's not always easy to integrate sexual pleasure and spiritual depth. David Deida helps single men and women and couples of every orientation turn sex into an erotic act of deep devotional surrender.

ISBN: 978-1-59179-273-4 / U.S. $16.95

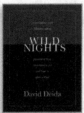

Wild Nights
Conversations with Mykonos about Passionate Love,
Extraordinary Sex, and How to Open to God

Meet Mykonos—scurrilous madman, and speaker of truth. A
recollection of a unique relationship between a student and an
extraordinary spiritual teacher.
ISBN: 978-1-59179-233-8 / U.S. $15.95

The Enlightened Sex Manual
Sexual Skills for the Superior Lover

The secret to enlightenment and great sex is revealed to be one and the
same in this groundbreaking manual for adventurous lovers. The ultimate
collection of skills for opening to the physical, emotional, and spiritual
rewards of intimate embrace.
ISBN: 978-1-59179-585-8 / U.S. $15.95

It's a Guy Thing
An Owner's Manual for Women

David Deida answers more than 150 of women's most asked questions
about men and intimacy.

Instant Enlightenment
Fast, Deep, and Sexy

David Deida offers a wealth of priceless exercises and insights to bring
"instant enlightenment" to the areas we need it most.
ISBN: 978-1-59179-560-5 / U.S. $12.95

AUDIO

Enlightened Sex
Finding Freedom & Fullness Through Sexual Union

A complete six-CD program to learn the secrets to transforming lovemaking into a spiritual gift to yourself, your lover, and the world.
ISBN: 978-1-59179-083-9 / U.S. $69.95

The Teaching Sessions: The Way of the Superior Man
Revolutionary Tools and Essential Exercises for Mastering the Challenges of Women, Work, and Sexual Desire

A spiritual guide for today's man in search of the secrets to success in career, purpose, and sexual intimacy—now available on four CDs in this original author expansion of and companion to the bestselling book.
ISBN: 978-1-59179-343-4 / U.S. $29.95

For information about all of David Deida's books and audio, visit **www.deida.info**.

To place an order or to receive a free catalog of wisdom teachings for the inner life, visit **www.soundstrue.com**, call toll-free **800-333-9185**, or write:
The Sounds True Catalog, PO Box 8010, Boulder CO 80306.

ABOUT THE AUTHOR

Acknowledged as one of the most insightful and provocative teachers of our time, bestselling author David Deida continues to revolutionize the way that men and women grow spiritually and sexually. His books have been published in more than twenty languages. His workshops on a radically practical spirituality have been hailed as among the most original and authentic contributions to the field of self-development currently available.

For more information about David Deida's books, audio, video, and teaching schedule, please go to **www.deida.info**.